The Grave of God

What are these churches now, but graves and sepulchres of God?

FRIEDRICH NIETZSCHE

Because of the nature of the historical development of her mode of being, the Church now stands in the way of her own progress.

I believe that, wherever we fail to dissociate ourselves voluntarily from this mode of being, the judgment of contemporary history will strike us like lightning and destroy us.

ALFRED DELP

THE
GRAVE
OF
GOD

Has the Church a Future?

ROBERT ADOLFS, O.S.A.

TRANSLATED BY N. D. SMITH

HARPER & ROW, PUBLISHERS
NEW YORK AND EVANSTON

The Grave of God is a translation of *Het graf van God. Heeft de Kerk nog Toekomst?* (Amboboeken, Utrecht, 1966)

Nihil Obstat:
Dr. A. F. Vermeulen OSA, Censor Deputatus

Imprimi Permittimus:
I. Mijnsbergen OSA, Prior Provincialis

Imprimatur:
Matthew A. P. J. Oomens, Vicarius Generalis.
Buscoduci, die 27 augusti 1966

Biblical quotations are from the Revised Standard Version of the Bible.

FIRST AMERICAN EDITION

LIBRARY OF CONGRESS CATALOG CARD NUMBER: 67-14940

Contents

Contents

Introduction

"RAPID change"—this phrase sums up, perhaps better than any other, the dynamic movement of modern society.

Change in the patterns of human society is, of course, something familiar to every generation. But in our own time changes are taking place with a rapidity that has never been known before. And this rapidly changing world compels us to think and act afresh and to live in constantly moving and readily adaptable patterns of behaviour.

For the Christian, the Church is a framework with its own norms of thought and action. But in our own time and in our present world completely new demands are being made on the Church. The Church is, after all, no peaceful garden in an otherwise turbulent world, but rather a vessel that is dependent on the waters in which it is sailing. And what happens to a vessel that suddenly and unexpectedly finds itself in the rapids? It is highly probable that it will sink. And so it is that nowadays so many different Christians can be heard expressing, in one way or another, some variation on the theme of "Lord, save us, we are sinking!"

Uneasiness, alarm and pessimism—these characterize the Christian of today. The signs of the times are unmistakable. Church Christianity is declining. The great decline in numbers is not in itself an exclusive sign of spiritual decline. What is really disturbing is the decreasing significance of Christianity to the world. It is openly stated that Christianity and the Church are no longer relevant in our secularized society. And this simply means that Christianity and the Church have very little meaning for *our* world. The proclamation of the Good News no longer brings the joy and liberation that is expected of it. Our modern world tries to resolve the great problems of life itself and is apparently helped more effectively in this by the human sciences and ideas of the modern age. Christianity is, of course, still held in respect, but in the sort of respect that is reserved for

7

venerable, but superseded social phenomena. The impression that Christianity gives is that it is becoming increasingly superfluous. And the result of this is that the Christian faith has almost been reduced to the level of a private opinion— an opinion which must be freely tolerated, but which cannot have, and cannot be allowed to have, any influence on the really important developments within our present society. This is undeniably a fact. The Christian faith plays hardly any part today, perhaps no part at all, in the really dynamic spheres of central importance in modern society—in science, politics, economics, business life, trade, technology and the social services. What is more, the Church is unprepared, clumsy and impotent in the face of such phenomena as urbanization, automation, the population explosion and the denationalization tendencies in politics and economics. These phenomena are now ineradicably with us and are pointing to a future of further rapid change.

The Church is no longer relevant to these or other developments that are taking place within society. That is perhaps why the Church means so little to the great masses in the world today. There are, of course, still certain spheres in which she still exerts an influence—in education, for example—but even there her witness is diminishing. The Church, then, would appear to be still relevant only in the clerical sphere, in family life and in the private life of those individuals who still believe. The Church has been pushed (or has perhaps withdrawn?) into the purely private orbit of life, in which we may include Sunday worship.

The urgent question in this connection is, what of the future? One wonders if the Church still has any meaning in the world today. But then, surely she has a universal task to fulfil in this world, an all-embracing task of redemption? Ought she not to be the salt, the light and the leaven in the world?[1] How, then, can she be all this now and *in the future*?

The remarkable thing is that this question is not simply a question that confronts the Roman Catholic Church only. The Protestant Churches are also faced with the same question. Dr J. M. van der Veen of the Dutch Reformed Church has written: "From the human point of view, the future does not look rosy for the Church and Christianity. . . . Radical changes are taking place in society and in men's lives and hearts. I need not describe these changes here. Let it suffice for me to say that continuous rationalization, industrialization and urbanization have created a new type of man, new patterns of social behaviour and new social structures, which *must* result in radical changes in the structures of the Churches and their parishes and congregations and in the ideas and the patterns of the behaviour of Christians."[2]

A recent Catholic article appeared with the significant title, "Where are the Church and Christianity going?"[3] Where are they going? In what direction? Or has the ship lost her rudder in the rapids of our modern world? And this is the same question as *has the Church a future?*

I can already hear some readers protesting—the situation is surely not so bad as that, the Council has brought about the renewal that was so necessary and the structural reforms and adaptations that were so desirable.

It is undeniable—the Council has been very important in the renewal and reform of the Church. There is, however, a serious danger of our overestimating the importance of the Council in this connection. A well-known English theologian has pointed out that the Council has demonstrated both the effectiveness and the limitations of institutionalized religion.[4] Essentially, the Council was little more than a professional discussion between administrators of the Church, but popular imagination turned it into a spiritual rebirth of the Church. History, however, has shown that spiritual rebirths simply do not take place at Councils. Apart from the openness, the new views and the freedom which the Council gave to the bishops, the main product of this Church assembly was a mass of verbal material which, in itself, is not really capable of creating a spiritual rebirth, let alone of changing men's hearts. Certainly the Council's decrees and constitutions provide us with a great number of norms and guiding lines which, in the long run, may well influence the moral behaviour of Christians. But the real limitation of the Coun-

9

cil was this—it was in principle an affair of the clergy, a fact to which I have already referred in a previous publication.[5] The clerical character of the Council emerged clearly from two matters which occupied a great deal of the attention of those who took part. I allude to the collegiality of the bishops and the renewal of the liturgy. What layman can really be terribly concerned about the complicated theological and jurisdictional relationships between the bishops, relationships which were designated by the word "collegiality", quite apart from the fact that, even now, the clergy still does not know how collegiality ought in fact to function? Priestly professionalism is nowhere more clearly revealed than in the recent liturgical reforms and the introduction of the language of the people. In the very nature of things, liturgy means a great deal to the clergy, but the number of lay people who are really interested in liturgical renewal is relatively small. Indeed, it is true to say that very many of the faithful still only "attend" Mass—they are present as outsiders. The translated and adapted liturgical rites are, as far as their form is concerned, still based on a Roman Byzantine court ceremonial that was designed for the élite to participate in and the majority to watch. The renewal of the liturgy is therefore most successful in the case of small, élite groups, especially those which interpret the restrictive regulations rather more freely. A popularized liturgy soon becomes banal. I do not wish to belittle the liturgical renewal in any way, but to acknowledge that its significance is limited is only realistic. What is more, a great deal of confusion as well as good has resulted from it inside the Church. And the liturgy has very little apostolic value in modern society as a means of Christian appeal.

Did the Council then succeed at all in renewing theology and thus, indirectly, the life of faith? Certainly many theologians came forward boldly with new ideas and made an important contribution to the renewal of Christian thought. A deeper meaning was given to the teaching about the Church herself, especially in the decree on ecumenism. But at the same time the shortcomings and limitations of Catholic theology emerged very clearly. Robert Kaiser has observed that ultimately the views of the "theologians on the march" fitted in neatly with those of the bishops.[6] In fact, the theologians showed themselves to be *apologists* of the Church. They defended their most venturesome ideas by using complicated arguments to show that what they were proposing was completely in accordance with the Church's previous statements or at least not in conflict with these statements. In short, the Council was not the place for radically new theology. Questions which had a direct bearing on concrete modern problems came off—to put it mildly—very badly (the decree on means of communication) or were removed from the agenda (the ethics of marriage and celibacy).

The great achievement of the Council and of the so-called *aggiornamento* was that attention was drawn to principles by means of which the Church could be structurally adapted in the future, with the result that she would at least no longer give the impression of being an antiquated monument among contemporary secular institutions. This structural adaptation has by no means been accomplished yet, but at least the principles exist, and the possibility of applying these principles.

And so we come back to the question, has the Church a future in the modern world? A question which, incidentally, was not raised at the Council. What, however, was raised was the need to adapt the Church structurally and in so doing to reorganize her so that her preaching would be more effective in contemporary human society. But, although the need to adapt the Church structurally from time to time and to bring her up to date (that is, the need for *aggiornamento*) was acknowledged, it was assumed without question that she would continue to exist with her basic form unchanged, for had not Christ himself said, "I am with you always, to the close of the age" (Matt. 28. 20)? The Church, thus assured that all would go well, could thus confidently face all crises, for she would always continue to exist and would overcome all difficulties. *Christus vincit*!

I believe, however, that Christ spoke these words in the

first place to his apostles and then, going further than the apostles, probably also addressed them to all those who were to be called together in faith. What he did not say, however, was, I am with *this* institution in *this* form always, to the close of the age. The Jesuit Alfred Delp saw this problem clearly with an insight made more acute by suffering. Shortly before dying a martyr's death in a concentration camp, he wrote: "Because of the nature of the historical development of her mode of being, the Church now stands in the way of her own progress. I believe that, wherever we fail to dissociate ourselves voluntarily from this mode of being, the judgment of contemporary history will strike us like lightning and destroy us."

Therefore I maintain—without false anxiety—that it is not only permissible but also necessary to ask the question, has the Church a future? In this book, I propose first of all to examine more closely the situation within which a question of this kind was able to arise. Then I shall analyse the question itself. Finally, I shall make an attempt to answer it. The fact that this answer will, in a certain sense, be negative, is bound to disturb some readers. But the consequences of this answer are not entirely without hope for the future.

This book is addressed to everyone who is, at the present time, anxious about the meaningful continued existence of the Church and Christianity. And because the question I have asked goes far beyond the confines of the Roman Catholic Church, the book is also addressed to all churches who confess Jesus Christ as the Lord and Redeemer of the world.

ROBERT ADOLFS, O.S.A.

I

The Situation of the Question

FIFTY, or even twenty years ago, Christians would have regarded the question, Has the Church a future? as meaningless and would probably have doubted the orthodoxy of the questioner himself. The mere fact that this question can be asked—often, perhaps, hesitantly—in our own time, clearly indicates that we are living in a situation of uncertainty and crisis.

How was it possible for such a situation to arise within the Christianity of the Church? Many attempts have already been made to interpret the phenomena of Christianity in crisis. In this chapter, I shall refer to only two of these attempts to understand the essence of the problem of our present situation. The first of these tendencies is known as the "death of God" movement because it traces the essence of our problem back to a crisis in the Christian idea of God.

A. THE PROBLEM OF GOD

The cry "God is dead" is not so very new. The philosopher Nietzsche used this phrase as long ago as 1882 in his book, *Die fröhliche Wissenschaft*, putting it in the mouth of a madman (*der tolle Mensch*) who proclaimed the death of God:

> Have you not heard of the madman who lit a lamp in broad daylight and ran up and down the market place shouting incessantly, "I'm looking for God! I'm looking for God!" But, because many of the people who were standing there did not believe in God, he aroused a good deal of mirth. Has he gone astray? one said. Is he lost, like a child? said another. Or is he hiding from us? Is he afraid of us? Has he gone on board ship? Is he emigrating?

They were all asking each other questions and laughing. But the madman thrust in between them and fixed them with his eyes. "Where is God?" he shouted. "I'll tell you! We have killed him—you and I! We are all his murderers! But how have we done it? How could we drink the sea dry? Who gave us the sponge to wipe away the horizon? What did we do when we uncoupled the earth from its sun? Where is the earth moving to now? Where are we moving to? Away from all suns? Are we not running incessantly? Backwards, sideways and forwards, in all directions? Is there still an above and a below? Are we not wandering through an infinite nothing? Is not the void yawning ahead of us? Has it not become colder? Is it not more and more night? Do the lamps not have to be lit during the day? Do we hear nothing of the noise of the gravediggers who are burying God? Do we smell nothing of the decomposition of God? The gods are decomposing! God is dead! God is dead! And we have killed him!..."[1]

At the end of Nietzsche's prophetic account, it is clear that no one understands the madman and Nietzsche makes him say: "I have come too soon! My time has not yet come. This terrible event is still coming." Is it possible that Nietzsche will be proved right in our own time? For, in 1961, his cry was heard again—this time from the lips of the sober American religious sociologist, Gabriel Vahanian. And his book was called *The Death of God*.[2] In it we read that the Church's idea of God was the product of an encounter between primitive Christianity and Greek civilization. The image of God is therefore an "idol" which has, moreover, become meaningless in our secular culture—neutralized by over-exposure, it is in fact usually rejected, therefore God is dead and will, for the time being, remain dead.

In the same year—1961—the theme of the death of God occurred again in a book by the American theologian William Hamilton:[3] "When we speak of the death of God, we speak not only of the death of the idols or the falsely objectivized being in the sky; we speak as well of the death in us of any power to affirm any of the traditional images of God . . . and wonder whether God himself has gone." Barely two years later, the southern United States were startled by a publication from the pen of the theologian Thomas Altizer,[4] a professor at Emory University in Atlanta, who wrote: "The moment has arrived to engage in a radical quest for a new mode of religious understanding. The first requirement of such a quest is a forthright confession of the death of the God of Christendom. We must recognize that the death of God is a historical event: God has died in *our* time, in *our* history and in *our* existence."[5]

Finally, there appeared in 1963 the difficult book by Paul van Buren,[6] a theologian of the school of linguistic analysis, who affirmed that the *word* "God" was dead. God, van Buren maintained, was a meaningless word, because it appeared to indicate a reality that could not in any way be verified and therefore could not function in a language which was in any way concerned with anything.

After considering all these statements, the unprepared reader will by now perhaps be wondering whether these theologians have gone mad. Or has Nietzsche been shown to be right? Are these theologians voicing an experience that is alive in the heart of Christianity itself? Also, is it not remarkable that the theme of the death of God occurs more or less explicitly in the work of the great writers and artists of today—in, for example, the films of Ingmar Bergman, the novels of Albert Camus and in Samuel Beckett's *Waiting for Godot*?

The Religious Crisis

It is, of course, possible for the slightly disturbed Catholic to say that these "death of God" theologians are simply muddle-headed Protestants and that the modern literary and artistic expressions simply reflect a general cultural decline.

But the Catholic who really believes this is clearly unaware of the fact to which I referred in the introduction to this book—the fact that Christianity is at present involved in a serious religious crisis, a crisis which cuts across all the Church's modalities and is revealed in all of them. The uneasiness and uncertainty that have taken deep root in the hearts of so many Christians frequently show themselves as sombre pessimism and this pessimism has in turn infected faith itself.

In the first place, many of the traditional, although secondary practices of the faith have disappeared. Secondly, the meaning of many important aspects of Christianity has been questioned—the Church's moral teaching, the absolute nature of her dogmatic statements, her sacramental practice, the real presence of Christ in the Eucharist, the Bible as the Word of God, the Church as an institution, the historicity of Christ and now, finally, the existence of God. All this has caused considerable alarm and makes one wonder whether we are not confronted with a veritable explosion of disbelief and an age in which God is completely forsaken.

Indeed, disbelief would appear to characterize our present age. I am not referring principally here to the cultural climate of present-day atheistic humanism, but to that almost intangible disbelief within Christianity that is so difficult to get hold of. If only it were an openly rebellious disbelief! But no, it is an almost imperceptible loss of faith, a silent falling away, a quiet indifference. It is a slowly maturing disbelief in the minds of men who have discovered that they can be men in the fullest sense without religious faith. It is a kind of positive indifference which shakes itself loose from faith by a positive acceptance of the worldly realities—work, science, art and politics are worth while in themselves and man can so fill his life with them that the Church, even God, become redundant.[7]

This positive indifference can be found everywhere at the higher levels of society today. At the lower levels of society and frequently among young people this indifference takes a rather more negative form. The so-called proletariat is to a very great extent a-religious and a-spiritual and forms, of course, a disturbingly large section of any community. In general, this group is quite indifferent to religion. Those who

16

belong to it have alarmingly little idea of what constitutes a norm and are almost exclusively interested in consumption —their values do not usually extend far beyond the easy earning of money and the purchase of luxury goods with it.

Is then the expression "God is dead" really so strange when once we realize that he has in fact died in the hearts of so many men? But we are bound to reassure ourselves at once with the remark, "But we are serious Christians—we still believe." In this context, the little word "still" is very significant. Yes, we still believe, but for how long? And so many very sincere believers are tormented by deep uncertainty and fear as they watch the apparently inviolable ground on which they have based their faith since childhood crumbling away beneath their feet. Indeed, many thinkers are of the opinion that the problem of God, both within the Church and outside it, constitutes the essence of the problem of our own time.

The Idea of God

God as a problem—this is not a new observation. Throughout the whole of the eighteenth and nineteenth centuries, the problem of God was the subject of philosophical and theological discussion at a high level. I need only mention here the names of Kant, Feuerbach, Schleiermacher, Troeltsch, Marx, Nietzsche and Freud. But what did ordinary Christians know about these learned discussions? There was a sense of security within the walls of the churches and the ordinary Christian could wrap himself in an unconditional (and uncritical) surrender to God's word (fundamentalism) or seek refuge in an individualistic devotion to Jesus (pietism). There was perhaps a certain amount of uneasiness among the clergy, but the ordinary people of God could continue calmly on their pilgrimage, unconscious of any threat of danger and thus quite unprepared for the crisis which was bound to come. It is possible to say that Bishop Robinson's little book broke through a scientific barrier and a Church barrier at the same time. The problem of God suddenly became the property of the world press and in this way the questionable property of the ordinary man in the street. We are still living in a state of shock brought about by *Honest to God*. Neither the theologians nor the clergy were in any way prepared for the sudden religious storm caused by this book and were consequently unable to move a finger to calm it.

It is therefore quite possible to say that the problem of God has quite rapidly become a universal problem for the Christian in our own time. This does not mean that God is dead, but that the problem of God now exists for many Christians in that the existence of God and the reality of God as something experienced in this world have been seriously called into question. In other words, God is no longer accepted by all Christians simply as a matter of course. Quite suddenly, we have made the startling discovery that the spheres in which God was previously so easily discernible have become narrowed down. At first it was said that God was concealing himself from us in our present age. In itself, however, this "concealment" of God gives no indication of a religious crisis, especially as it is a biblical theme that occurs particularly in Isaiah and the Psalms. "Concealment" is, moreover, still a form of presence. Then, quite suddenly, the phrase "the absence of God" was heard in religious circles. And this is more or less the same idea that the theologians whom I have quoted earlier on have attempted to express, although in a more striking way, in the phrase "God is dead".

I must now try to interpret this disturbing and negative phrase. The question is, what is the reason for this reference, within Christian circles, to the death of God? For the time being at least, the answer must be, the positive acceptance of the *secularization* of our Western society, which has sharply increased in this century.

Secularization

This is a word that requires some clarification. We are always coming up against it, but are seldom told what it really means. The difficulty, of course, is that secularization is a phenomenon that is still taking place and cannot therefore be fully defined. The word is derived from the Latin *saeculum*, which means this world, this age. We could therefore define secularization as the liberation of man from all religious, supernatural, mythical and metaphysical explanations of the world, after which he seeks to explain his world and himself-in-the-world by examining the legality of this world (the sciences) and by analysing his own existence (existentialism). It is, however, clear that this definition requires further explanation.

Primitive man tried to explain his existence and the mystery of the world that surrounded him in *mythical* accounts. Man's earliest testimony of his primitive faith and moral wisdom was in the form of myths. Without going further into this here, let me give two examples—the division of the world into three levels (heaven, earth and hell) and the personification of good and evil (good and bad gods, angels and demons) both have mythical origins.

At a later stage, philosophical thought developed and this resulted in *metaphysical* thought. Metaphysics arose because man was dissatisfied with the world as he actually saw it. The ancient Greek philosophers were the first to attempt to transcend the many forms of this world, endeavouring to answer the great question, what is behind the sensorily perceptible forms of our reality? All realities are similar in that they *are*; the metaphysicians therefore looked for the deeper meaning of these beings, in other words, for the *essence* of things. From the very beginning, then, metaphysics made a division between two worlds—the world that is perceived by the senses and the real world that is beyond the senses. Plato was the classic exponent of this view, maintaining that man can find no meaning in the visible world, which only points to the (as yet) invisible basic forms of a higher "being", the being of the world of ideas, that is, the real world. Our world is therefore only a reflection of this higher reality, the real world of ideas.[8] This metaphysical explanation of the world and man has, in its many variations,

19

conditioned the whole philosophical and theological thought of our own Western civilization.

It is therefore very important to realize that Christianity has been very deeply influenced both by mythical and by metaphysical thought. The Bible originated in societies which thought mythically. In the third and fourth centuries, Christianity was strongly influenced by Greek metaphysical thought. The great controversies about the dogma of Christ were finally settled with the help of concepts derived from Greek philosophy, and the scholastic theology of the Middle Ages was to a very great extent based on the philosophy of Aristotle.

Let two examples from the Nicene Creed suffice to illustrate this—"Who for us men . . . *came down from heaven*", which clearly reflects mythical influences, and "*consubstantial* with the Father", which shows the influence of metaphysics.

The problematical elements of the Christian statements on faith and even more of the Christian proofs of God can now be seen in a clearer light. The Christian witness is, so to speak, enshrined within the framework of mythical and metaphysical ideas. A society in the process of secularization —one which rejects both myth and metaphysics—finds Christianity and its proofs of the existence of God incomprehensible, part of an outmoded phase of development, and no longer credible in our own age.

Liberation from Religion

Secularization also means the liberation of man and his environment from the claims of religion and the religious view of life. The common secular view is that religion and religious phenomena belong to the immature stage in man's development. According to the religious view of the world, everything that was inexplicable was interpreted as sacral. For religious man, the world was full of mysterious, sacred and magic elements—it was, in other words, full of gods. With the coming of Christianity, it was asserted that the Christian faith had purified religion, had reduced these gods,

which were often very much a part of this world, to one
heavenly God and had included the magic and sacred
elements and raised them to the level of a sacramental
system.

Now, more and more theologians are beginning to question whether Christianity is really a religion at all and to
wonder whether we ought not to leave the religious stage
behind us and, following Bonhoeffer, think in terms of a
Christianity without religion. According to this view, which
in fact applies secularization to Christianity, Christianity is
not a religion, but a faith (as an orientation of human existence) in Jesus and in his gospel in which the eschatological
event of the fullness of time is proclaimed. Christianity has
therefore to be liberated from its "religious character". Some
of the theologians who incline to this view even maintain
that this secularization of Christianity has its roots in and
is thus already provided in the message of the Old Testament
and the gospels.

In this context, it is understandable that we can speak,
in a positive sense, about the death of God. The god of religion and the god of the philosophers (that is, the theism of
the natural teaching about God) is the god who is outside
our verifiable reality, a god both of myth and of metaphysics,
a god about whom profound discussions can be held and
whose existence we can approach via the scholastic proofs.
These theologians do not deny the possibility of the existence of such a god, but they do maintain that he is no
longer relevant to our world. They add that it is also open
to doubt whether this god is still the Father of Jesus
Christ and the god of grace (van Buren). It is therefore
possible to speak, in this sense, of an a-theistic Christianity.[9]

Thus, secularization means the disappearance of the
mythical, the metaphysical and the religious idea of God.
What have we left, then? some readers will ask. This surely
means the end of Christianity! The "death of God" theologians, however, claim that the very opposite is true. For
them, secularization is a necessary purification, a liberation

of Christianity from the stranglehold of myth, metaphysics and religion.

In fact, the phrase "the death of God" points, within the context of what they have written, to these theologians' deep concern for God as believers. They confidently expect that God will once again become relevant in our world, and in a way that is as yet not known to us. So far, they choose to say very little about this, since the way in which God will appear will not become clear to us until we have all experienced and brought about the death of God. Some of them, however, see a little light already.

Altizer believes that this light will break through when the sacred, the symbolic and the mythical can be interpreted anew and in such a way that it once again becomes relevant to our present-day sensibilities.

Hamilton says that, in experiencing the absence of God, we need not be entirely without hope because God will appear to us again within an authentically Christian "waiting". In the meantime, we have once again to give ourselves over entirely to the inspiration of Jesus and his way of life. Our encounter with Jesus takes place in our loving contact with our spiritually and materially troubled fellow man.

Vahanian has sought to find a new appearance of God by re-interpreting the concept of transcendence. For him, transcendence does not mean that God exists in another world that is infinitely distant, a world beyond our own world and therefore beyond our grasp, but that he is, on the contrary, immanent in, very close to our historical reality.

Finally, van Buren wishes to eliminate the word "God" from our vocabulary. It may allude to the Father of whom the man Jesus of Nazareth spoke. Jesus himself seemed to suggest that we should not look for the "essence of the Father", since everything that we know about him was made public in Jesus. Jesus is the really free man and a liberating and renewing effect emanates from him. The gospel is the good news about a free man whose freedom is still contagious and still able to lead us to true humanity.

Critical Review

It will be clear from the foregoing that the problem of God has arisen as a result of a confrontation between the concept of God that is current in the churches today and the secular thought and understanding of modern man. The God of Church Christianity has to a very great extent lost all relevance and credibility in the world today. The thinkers who express this in the statement "God is dead" are not simply expressing a contemporary experience—they are also, and with good reason, pointing to a certain untenability of the traditional idea of God. We must now examine their opinions to see whether or not they are in fact completely right.

In the first place, there is, in the phrase "God is dead", an echo of a fully justified opposition to the so-called objectivization of God within traditional Christian teaching, in other words, the making of God the object of our knowledge, the end-product of metaphysical reasoning.

In opposing this objectivization of God, certain contemporary theologians, influenced by existential thought from the standpoint of the human subject, have gone to the other extreme and have fallen into the trap of subjectivization. But, as Vahanian has correctly observed, "believing" is a movement which tends to reconcile and bring together the subject, man, and the object, God. God, however, has been divorced from believing and has consequently been objectivized and situated somewhere "up there". Hamilton and van Buren have, after rejecting the objectivization of God, not been entirely successful in avoiding the tendency to situate God simply and solely within our sensorily perceptible world at a level of encounter between human beings that is based on the inspiration of Christ. However valuable this may be, it does neglect an essential dimension. (See the following section.)

The "death of God" theologians are right, however, to dispose of all self-assured knowledge concerning the existence and essence of God. Compared with the writers of the inflated theological treatises of a later period, Thomas Aquinas was a very modest thinker who is revealed as a pious agnostic in the following quotation from the *De veritate* : "What God really is will always be hidden from us, and this is the supreme knowledge which we can have of God in this life —that we know that he transcends every idea that we can ever form of him".

Consequently, the cry "God is dead" is a call to theologians to devote more attention to the reluctance and the awe with which the Old Testament writers spoke of God. Reverence prompted them to avoid using the name "Yahweh" as far as they could. "Yahweh" was not for them a name of an objective Supreme Being, but a form of address, an appeal, a name to be invoked, entreated and praised. "Yahweh" did not disclose his objective being, but revealed himself in the history of a people. The liberation of Israel from slavery in Egypt was the revelation of Yahweh's love and concern for his people and his disclosure of the grace of election. It is this divine revelation, which opens up a new perspective on to history and thus on to our personal lives as well, that the "death of God" theologians are anxious to emphasize. They are convinced that the mythical, metaphysical and religious god must die before we can once again be really open to the real revelation of God.

The Lost Dimension

In my opinion, however, the "death of God" theologians are guilty of one great failing. They have greeted secularization with altogether too much enthusiasm and too few reservations. The question is, are the mythical, metaphysical and religious explanations of the world stages in the history of man's conscious development, his process of humanization, which belong definitively to the past as outmoded "ways of seeing" and interpretations of the world? Has nothing been brought up, in the sense of explicit experiences, in the mythical, metaphysical and religious modes of thinking and seeing that is of value as reality for the world we live in? Rudolf Bultmann has already pointed out that the mythical view of the world is, in its original, primitive form, incomprehensible and meaningless to modern man. His aim, in "demythologizing", was not to do away with myths, but to "translate" what they contained into modern (existential) terms. Altizer also aims to reinterpret the primitive experience of the sacred. Modern secular man, in his aversion to minimalizing the reality of this world by "believing" in another world that is beyond this one, a supernatural, transcendental world beyond the senses, has developed a blind spot in his vision. Because of this, he tends to ignore the profound existential experience of previous generations and to overestimate his own mode of seeing.

Is there not, after all, a *growth* in this world towards a higher condition of human consciousness? Despite the inhumanity of wars, trials, cruelty and self-seeking egotism, mankind has constantly struggled towards a fuller and deeper humanity, welcoming and eagerly seizing hold of everything that can renew and humanize his existence as real progress. But how is it that the achievement of greater humanity, of greater opportunities in life, of more freedom, goodness, peace and happiness in the world has, throughout history, always been a hard struggle? Has all this simply been deduced from analysing our own existence in the world? I do not think so! Man might just as well have chosen to follow the course of egotism, loving only himself and hating his fellowmen—and indeed, that is undeniably a course which he is always tending to follow, and to which he again and again returns. No, he can follow the course of true progress only because he is, in some way or another (and words are totally inadequate here), "called". He is somehow addressed, summoned or challenged—he is, so to speak, aware of a mysterious "voice" which "calls" him. This is not a facile mysticism, but a genuine existential experience which cannot be adequately described in words. Man has always experienced this "call" as something that comes from another dimension, from a sphere that is different from the world of his own immediate experience. Mythical man expressed this experience in his own primitive manner, the metaphysician referred to a transcendental world beyond the senses and religious man called it "god". Is it wrong to suppose that Jesus called it "the Father"? In our present situation, we must perhaps avoid using the word "God". But perhaps we must learn to cultivate an attitude of listening and waiting receptivity towards the mystery that "calls", "addresses" and "invites" us.

The situation within which the question, has the Church a future? could arise is apparently characterized by a crisis which has its centre in the Christian idea of God. This crisis had its origin in the rigid dogmatism of the churches. These had clung for too long to mythical, metaphysical and religious formulae without constantly reinterpreting these formulae so as to give them a meaning that would arouse faith in each successive generation of Christians. In addition, God was objectivized and thus situated, as an object, outside the sphere of our own reality. This objectivization of God had very grave consequences, since a God so conceived could be misused by a church with opportunist aims.[10] This misuse of an objectivized God has indeed often occurred in past centuries, for example, to justify man's oppression of his fellows and inhuman situations. As Bonhoeffer has pointed out, this God has been used to fill in the gaps in our knowledge and our abilities, to justify wars and bloodshed ("It is God's will!") and to defend the partisan interests of the churches. Further back in history, he was used to justify the feudal system and, more recently, he was seen, not without justification, by the nineteenth-century Communists as the protector of the capitalist system and the *bourgeoisie*.

In this context, it is, however, open to question whether the problem of God is in itself at the heart of our present critical situation or whether it is only a symptom of this situation.

In a very illuminating article about the problem of God in Robinson, Professor Schillebeeckx has expressed the opinion that

all the social surveys conducted by religious sociologists

26

(and our own concrete experience) show clearly that the chief difficulty is not the problem of God, nor even Christ, but the Church. The question that is asked is, why does the Church mediate between us and God or Christ? A rather forced survey conducted among the *nouvelle vague* in France (that is, young people between the ages of eighteen and thirty) has revealed that only 9% of this group calls itself consciously atheistic, 5% is hesitant (agnostic) and 13% is non-practising Catholic with atheistic tendencies, whereas 73% admits to a vague belief in God as the ground of all being, even though the members of this group are not practising Christians. The difficulties experienced in "secularized France" in connection with religion are therefore not really concerned with God or Christ, but with the Church and its character and function. The same picture emerges from several English surveys that I have consulted briefly. [Robinson] has therefore not touched on the real centre of uncertainty with regard to faith—the Church.[11]

Although an analysis of the "death of God" movement can provide very valuable insights into the deeper causes of the crisis of contemporary Christianity, it is very much open to doubt whether this movement has really gone to the heart of our problem. There are, moreover, indications which suggest that the main difficulty is to be found in the form and the mode of existence of the Church.

B. THE PROCLAMATION OF THE CHRISTIAN MESSAGE

However, it is possible that we are too hasty in coming to conclusions. In recent years, powerful voices have been heard in theological circles which stress, not so much the problem of the Church as such, as the existence of a critical situation in the proclamation of the Christian message. This message is preached in such a way in our modern secular society that it has become unintelligible. The jargon of the Church is possibly still understood in elevated ecclesiastical circles familiar with the traditional teaching of the Church, but in the world outside it is regarded at best as pious but irrelevant.

This has resulted in strenuous efforts being made on various theological fronts to renew the Church's preaching. A genuine concern for this preaching has led to the emergence of three very interesting theological schools which have become extremely important in modern Christian thought. As will become evident, there is a clear connection between these attempts to renew the proclamation of the message and what was discussed in the first part of this chapter under the heading "The problem of God". Furthermore, there are also remarkable similarities between these three theological tendencies, in that they all, to some extent, draw their inspiration from contemporary philosophies.

These three movements must now be briefly discussed, in order that we may have a better idea of the situation within which our original question arose.

(a) Demythologization

"Demythologizing" originated with Rudolf Bultmann. While he was serving as a Forces chaplain in the trenches during the First World War he made the painful discovery that the traditional Christian message had a kind of primitive fairy-tale magic which "came off" in the nursery, but which meant absolutely nothing in the turmoil of war. The question as to how the Christian message could be preached in a meaningful manner to contemporary man continued to haunt him, but it was not until the Second World War (1942) that he published his ideas about demythologizing the New Testament.

Very briefly, Bultmann's demythologization is a method whereby the mythological concept of man, that is, man's understanding of himself, a concept which is implicit in the New Testament, is interpreted in such a way that it can be understood by contemporary man and can compel him to make a decision, the decision of faith, which intimately concerns his *own* existence.[12]

Bultmann, therefore, did not aim to do away with the mythology of the New Testament, but to reinterpret it. He regarded mythology as an authentic expression of man's

28

understanding of himself in the world in which he was living and, in the case of the New Testament, this world was that of the Hellenistic East at the beginning of our era. The mythical ideas of this world reflected the conception of man that was current at that time, but this mythology, which saw the world as populated by angels, devils and spirits and as full of miracles, has since been superseded and has little or no meaning now in our modern world. Bultmann therefore concluded that the proclamation of the gospel ought not at the same time to be a proclamation of the mythical view of man and the world that is contained in the New Testament. To put it quite simply, modern Christians cannot swallow this mythology any more. Bultmann consequently believed that it was necessary, for the purpose of proclaiming the gospel today, to examine this ancient mythology with the greatest care, to discover the conception of human existence that was implicit in it and then to interpret this conception of man in modern terms. This modern terminology was, in Bultmann's view, available in the terminology of present-day existential philosophy, and Bultmann consequently made considerable use of the analysis of human existence (*Daseinsanalyse*) provided by the philosopher Martin Heidegger in his book *Sein und Zeit*.[13]

The use of philosophical terms is not unknown in theology. The scholastic theologians of the Middle Ages accepted without difficulty the achievements of philosophy. But Bultmann was sharply criticized, in orthodox Church circles especially, for his attempts to demythologize the gospel—it was feared that the influence of modern, "pagan" philosophy would result in the gospel losing its lustre. Moreover, frequent misunderstandings have arisen in connection with his demythologization, which can, after all, be interpreted as meaning an attempt to do away altogether with the mythological terminology of the New Testament. It should, however, be stressed that this was in no way Bultmann's intention. His theology, of which demythologization is, in fact, only one aspect, is also fairly difficult to understand and certainly does not lend itself to popularization. He has, however, succeeded in introducing a new and dynamic element into theology as a whole and the study of the New Testament in particular and in inspiring with new hope those who believe that the gospel can still be preached in a relevant manner to modern secular man.

(b) *The "Answer" Theology*

Paul Tillich is another theologian who has attempted to make the proclamation of the gospel intelligible to modern man. In his view, all theology has a historical character. Authentically Christian theology must, according to Tillich, satisfy two requirements—it must provide an exposition of the truth of the Christian message and at the same time an interpretation of this truth for each new generation. All theology and all proclamation of the message must therefore always take into account the situation of the man to whom the message is being proclaimed.

Modern man is estranged from the Church, the Bible and faith. The Christian message no longer appeals to man today because its proclamation no longer arises from the contemporary human situation and is no longer addressed to this situation. The Christian attitude has been overshadowed by the idea of possessing the eternal truth of the Christian message. As a consequence, theologians have, in their anxiety not to minimize this eternal truth that was, so to speak, in their possession, identified its formulation with the theological achievements of the past and with traditional concepts and conclusions. The preaching of the Christian message has therefore been a continued attempt to impose this traditional "possession" on modern man, whose situation is entirely new and entirely different. In other words, the eternal truth of Christianity has been confused with an expression of this truth that was conditioned by historical circumstances.

Tillich's starting-point for his theology, then, is a listening to contemporary man. How does modern man understand his own humanity and his situation in this world? In order to find out about this, Tillich has made extensive use of modern existential philosophy and in particular of the analysis of human existence as developed by Heidegger. But he has not limited himself simply to contemporary philosophy. In order to understand who this man to whom the Christian message must be directed really is, he has also examined literature, pictorial art, drama, modern psychology and other spheres. Tillich insists that theologians will not be able to discover what *questions* modern man is asking until they have some knowledge of this man and his situation. His theology is therefore known as the "answer" theology, because it attempts to answer the questions that are implicit in man's situation. In other words, if the proclamation of the Christian message is to overcome its continued alienation from the human situation, it must take man's needs, aspirations and questions into consideration. If the Christian message does not do this, it can no longer be regarded as a message, since a message that relates to nothing is not a message. There must therefore be an interaction, a reciprocal relationship or a correlation between the Christian message and the human situation in which this message has to be proclaimed.[14]

Tillich has worked this out in great detail in the three volumes of his *Systematic Theology*, a work which, like Bultmann's theology, is by no means easy for the ordinary reader to understand, but which has indirectly had a great influence on the development of a more relevant preaching of the gospel to modern, secular man.

(c) *The Method of Linguistic Analysis*

The most recent attempt to renew the proclamation of the Christian message has been made by the American theologian Paul van Buren in his book, *The Secular Meaning of the Gospel*.[15] Van Buren has tried to make this proclamation intelligible to modern man "whose job, community, and daily life are set in the context of the pragmatic and empirical thinking of industry and science".[16] This need caused van Buren to turn to the movement within the philosophy of the English-speaking world that is known as logical positivism (Wittgenstein, G. E. Moore), although he is less interested in the philosophy of logical positivism as such than in the method of linguistic analysis that has resulted from it. This is an investigation into the way in which language functions, into how words and statements function in their actual use, and the method can, it is claimed, lead to our establishing whether statements are meaningful or meaningless. Linguistic analysis is based on the initial assumption that, in thought, we are frequently bewitched by words and statements, without in fact knowing what they really mean. There is therefore an urgent need for a strictly scientific method of investigating our statements on a basis of their meaning. In the method of linguistic analysis, it is the so-called principle of verification which provides the criterion by which our words and statements are judged to be meaningful or without meaning. According to this principle, statements are true and meaningful if they can be experimentally or empirically verified. Thus, historical events can be empirically verified, but a supernatural world cannot, and is therefore meaningless.

Van Buren, then, is convinced that the Christian must arm himself with the method of linguistic analysis, which both reflects and throws light on the way in which we think and speak in our everyday lives. An empirically orientated attitude towards life characterizes our industrialized and technological society. In van Buren's opinion, Christians living in an industrialized society are well advised to remain open to this attitude, so long as they take seriously the problem of "how modern man thinks".[17]

As far as theology was concerned, one great difficulty that logical positivism presented was that, to begin with at least, all theological statements were regarded as meaningless because they could not be verified. Van Buren, however, was able to make use of a later development in the principle of verification, which was introduced when it became clear that the original, rigorous application of this principle was no longer tenable. To begin with, logical positivists had thought of language far too much as an entity of words and statements, each possessing, with an almost mathematical precision, only one meaning. Later, however, they discovered the existence, within any language, of a great number of what they called "language games", which were different in content and thus could not simply be used interchangeably. (For example, the language game of biology is different from that of politics or from that of love.) Included among one of these language games is language arising from so-called "discernment situations". Such a situation exists, for example, when a young man suddenly falls in love with a girl whom he has known for a long time. Precisely what happens in a discernment situation cannot be verified, but the fact that some kind of discernment situation has taken place can be verified from a person's subsequent actions and use of language.

These rather technical expositions of linguistic analysis are necessary if van Buren's intentions are to be made clear. The question that he asks is, "How can a Christian, himself a secular person, understand the gospel in a secular manner?" In the first place, this question shows van Buren's concern that the gospel should be understood. Then he insists that we live in a secular society, that secularity is something that is present in every modern man, and therefore also in every Christian and that we have to accept this secularity. If we do this, then the gospel has also to be interpreted in a secular manner. One of the first and most startling conclusions that van Buren comes to is that all speaking about God is meaningless. "God" is a meaningless word because it cannot be empirically verified. Therefore, van Buren maintains, theo-logy, as a "teaching about God", is also meaningless. At first sight, this is a disturbing affirmation. But is it really so disturbing if we examine it more closely? Van Buren says that it is not, since a study of the history of theology reveals a primary concern for Christology. Van Buren therefore reduces theology to a teaching about Jesus of Nazareth. Using the principle of verification as the basis of his reasoning, he maintains that the point of departure for all "theology" must be the person of Jesus of Nazareth.

33

Jesus was a historical figure and as such can be verified. It is, of course, true that the history of Jesus of Nazareth is to some extent hidden from us because he comes to us from the gospels as he was seen and appreciated in the primitive Christian community. This is, however, not problematical, since the primitive Christian community saw Jesus in the light of the event of Easter which was, for the apostles and disciples, the great "discernment situation". The precise content of the discernment situation of the Easter event cannot be verified, but what can be established is that the apostles and disciples were different men afterwards, seeing Jesus and their own lives in a totally new perspective. In my opinion, van Buren has in this way secularized the meaning-content of the word "believe".

Jesus is also described by van Buren as a particularly free man. He was free of family ties, spoke with an authoritative freedom, acted with great freedom even with regard to the religious legislation of his own people and he was above all free for others. Through the discernment situation of the Easter event, this freedom had a contagious influence on the apostles and disciples, with the result that Jesus' freedom henceforth became the power and the norm of their own way of life (and this is clearly a secularization of the Christian doctrine of the redemption). This discernment situation, this seeing of the historical person, Jesus of Nazareth, in a new perspective, that of faith, is still taking place and leads to a situation of dedication and surrender to a way of life, of commitment, as van Buren calls it. The freedom of Jesus can therefore be contagious in our own time as well, provided that the Christian message is proclaimed in terms that are acceptable to modern, secular and empirically orientated man.

This very short summary of van Buren's book is, of course, very unfair to the author, and I can only assure the reader that the book is a serious work written with great care. It is a very difficult book to read, but it constitutes a serious attempt to break through the crisis in the proclamation of the gospel today with radical means. The very fact that such a difficult book—for anyone not trained in theology it is practically unreadable—has become a best-seller is a clear indication that modern man is looking eagerly for a new and relevant proclamation of the Christian message.

A critical appreciation of these three theological movements lies outside the scope of this chapter. But it should, for the time being, be noted that the proclamation of the Christian message of salvation, even if this is couched in modern terms, does not automatically lead to acceptance. The preaching of the gospel is always an infringement of the human constellation.

The Essence of the Problem   1405609

I have indicated in the foregoing sections one or two important aspects of the critical situation in which Christianity finds itself today. In the first part of this chapter, I discussed the far-reaching phenomenon of secularization. It is almost impossible to imagine the revolutionary effects of secularization on Christian thought. This world and this life have, until the present, been seen by Christians as unreal and sinful, a world to which the statement "Do not love the world" (1 John 2. 15) was applied. The real world of truth and purity was to be found on the other side of the grave—although it had its beginning here, the real life was otherworldly.

Secular thought is strongly opposed to this idea and affirms the very opposite—this is the real world and must be fully accepted. The whole problem known as the "Church and the World" is centred in an attempt to come to terms with this tendency towards secularization, which has led to a crisis in the Christian idea of God and of the existence of God. But whether the problem of God is really the essential problem of contemporary Christianity is open to doubt—it is more probably a symptom of a crisis in the churches.

Various attempts to penetrate to the heart of this problem have produced the following result—the proclamation of the Christian message is inadequate. This is the conclusion to which three leading modern theologians have come, each by a different path. And each of these theologians has tried to provide a solution. But even so, it is doubtful whether they have really penetrated to the heart of the matter. Is the proclamation of the gospel not the primary task of the Church? May not the conservative character of ecclesiastical institutions be the reason for preaching (and theology) becoming unintelligible in the modern, secular world?

What emerges again and again in the works of the theologians discussed in this chapter is that the Church should not, in the name of orthodoxy, simply continue to present her old, traditional teaching, but that she must be conscious of her mission as something that applies to all ages and, in continuity and in discontinuity with the past, constantly reinterpret the Christian message for each new generation.

Preaching and the promulgation of the gospel constitute an enormous task for the Church and constantly require her to exert herself to the limits of her powers. But, until the present, the Church has always thought in terms of a "deposit of faith", a sort of possession that had to be kept in her strong room and carefully guarded, with the result that her teaching acquired a trans-historical and absolute character and the gospel was interpreted in a manner that was associated with a past period of history.

The Church's teaching is out of tune with the modern age because the form itself of the Church is also a survival from a past age. This form has to be reinterpreted and refashioned in every new human and world situation. Everything points to the fact that it is almost certainly the form of the Church that is the real cause of the critical situation in which Christianity finds itself in the modern world. If the Church remains as she has been until the present (and this applies to the post-conciliar Church as well), then it may well be that she will become the grave of Christianity. This is a paradoxical thought, and one that we either cannot or will not accept. Where, then, has the Church failed? We must go further into this problem in the chapters that follow. Our original question, however, was concerned with the future of the Church. Now that we have briefly outlined the situation within which this question could arise, we must, then, consider first of all the meaning of the term "future" within the context of this question.

II

The Future

ANYONE who sets out to answer the question, Has the Church a future?, obviously claims to know something about the future—a claim which at once brings him face to face with difficulties. Prophesying the future is, to say the very least, an activity that is open to suspicion. There have been too many charlatans in this field and too many "prophets" over-endowed with fantasy and lacking in a sense of reality. Nonetheless, there is a long tradition of attempting to form some idea of the future, the optimists in this sphere fore-casting a utopian future, the pessimists, like Spengler, point-ing to a decline of the West. It is in none of these ways that I propose to speak about the future here.

Futurology

In our own time, we have witnessed the emergence of a new way of speaking about the future that is matter-of-fact, scientific and above all necessary. The need has arisen be-cause of a totally new phenomenon in the world—the enor-mously increased speed of developments. "Modern man is moving, geographically, socially and spiritually, more quickly and in a more all-embracing sense than ever before in his-tory."[1] This rapid human movement and change has been brought about especially by scientific and technical evolution. "500,000 years may have elapsed between the first man who used a stone as a tool and the first man who fashioned stones into axes and spear-heads. 5,000 years elapsed between the first blacksmith and the first locomotive engineer and only 130 between the locomotive engineer and the first pilot to fly a jet fighter at a speed faster than that of sound. This advance spanned several generations, but within our own lifetime we have experienced Otto Hahn's discovery in 1938

38

of a chain reaction in the nuclear fission of uranium and, only seven years later, the dropping of the atomic bomb on Hiroshima in 1945."[2]

The rapidity of developments in the modern world have forced men—industrialists, business men, politicians and scientists—to look at least twenty years ahead, if not more. The great word of our present age is "planning", but planning is impossible without some provisional analysis of future developments. For this reason, scientific institutes have already been set up which are exclusively concerned with the future. A new science has emerged—the science of futurology.[3]

This science, however, differs from the other sciences in that it leaves a far greater margin for unknown, uncertain and probable factors. But if our attitude towards the world of tomorrow is to be one of responsibility and preparedness, then a far-seeing strategy is an indispensable condition for every sphere of human thought and action. Analyses, prognoses and extrapolations of the present reality that is already in motion form the basis of this scientific study of the future. Although futurologists are aware that certain events, such as new discoveries, revolutions and wars—especially an atomic war—are unknowns which can change, transform or even put a stop to this movement of history, they are also firmly convinced that a beginning must be made now with strategical planning for the future.

It is, then, in this sense that I shall be speaking about the future. I am, moreover, impelled by the conviction that Christianity and the Church have to exist in the world of tomorrow and that the Church is still too dominated in her thinking by transcendental and other-worldly categories and too little concerned with man and society in this world, the world of the future. It is necessary to make this point here, although the problem will be dealt with in a later chapter.

Beyond the Revolutions

Before discussing the future of man and the world, however, something more has to be said about our view of history in connection with the present. The word "revolution" is often used with reference to our own age.[4] A revolution is a sudden and frequently violent action or intervention in the course of history which causes events to move in a new direction. Revolution is, of course, an all-embracing concept and can be applied to all spheres of human life. I shall consider it here in its broadest significance.

In my opinion, it is wrong to regard the developments of our own time (and the future) as revolutionary. I believe that, although the dynamism of the present is the product of revolutions, the revolutions themselves belong to the past. We use the word revolution because we have no other word available through which to designate the completely new phenomena within our present situation. And there is, in my view, no doubt that we are confronted now with a phenomenon in the history of man that has never been known before. It is therefore important to examine this new phenomenon and interpret it correctly.

Our present age is, as I have said, the product of a number of revolutions that took place in the past. The eighteenth and nineteenth centuries especially were characterized by revolutionary events that radically changed the course of history. I do not intend to discuss this recent history in detail here, but it is important to indicate briefly the various revolutions that took place in those centuries.

1. *The scientific revolution* was the most gradual of these revolutions. Perhaps the real beginning of this revolution in the thinking and "seeing" of (Western) man was the philosophy of Descartes. A new vision of the reality of the cosmos came into being and the earth and the forces that were latent in it became the object of intense study. Before this scientific revolution, man was helpless in the presence of the forces of nature. He felt himself to be abandoned to unknown cosmic forces which he did not understand and which frequently threatened him in his existence. He turned spontaneously to God for protection, believing that God controlled the natural world. Scientific thought meant a radical change in the way

40

man viewed the earth. The inner laws of nature were studied, the various sciences were differentiated, the cosmos lost its mysterious quality and became less threatening, and man suddenly felt himself to be in control of nature. The reality of this world was increasingly seen as something that was measurable and predictable. This vision continued to develop until it became the only possible view of the cosmic reality.

There is no doubt that this constituted the first great step towards secularization. Man had wrested from God some of the power that had hitherto always been regarded as his alone. The earth had lost its mysterious and sacred character.

2. *The social revolution* was the great event which took place at the end of the eighteenth century. The French Revolution is generally regarded as the great event in history in which this social change took place, in other words, in which the feudal structure of society that had endured for centuries was finally and violently destroyed. Man refused, at this point in history, to accept any longer the arbitrary oppression of the overwhelming majority of the people by a minority group, in this case, the aristocracy. At the same time, this social revolution resulted in the emergence of the democratic ideals of freedom and of the right of every man to at least minimum opportunities in life and of the recognition of the dignity of the human person. Today, accepting without reflection the democratic climate in which we live, we can only with difficulty imagine the enormous significance of this revolution in the pattern of life of the individual and society.

3. *The technical and industrial revolution* was the outcome of the practical application of the products of the natural sciences. One technical invention followed another in rapid succession. New sources of energy were discovered and harnessed to human productivity. These technical developments resulted in profound changes in the sphere of work—the crafts and manual labour which had persisted for centuries were replaced by machinery and the family and

cottage industries gave way to more and more highly organized labour in larger factory units. The technical revolution led, in other words, to industrialization and mass production—a development which has radically changed the whole face of our civilization in barely a hundred years.

4. *The social and economic revolution* was partly a consequence of the industrial revolution. Industrialization and mass production brought about a transformation in the hitherto primitive economy. The changed economic laws, such as the law of supply and demand, resulting from the new industrial process of production, were at first not clearly distinguishable. Very soon, however, the capitalist system emerged, in which the greatest possible freedom in trade, production and the creation of capital was encouraged. This new capitalist economy had far-reaching consequences at the social level, creating a new form of society which had a great deal in common with the earlier feudal pattern of human relationships. Capital became the possession of a small group of men. The factory workers, on the other hand, who formed the great majority, found that their efforts were, relatively speaking, only meagrely rewarded. The small capitalist upper class gained almost total power, whereas the industrial proletariat, labouring frequently in sub-human conditions, remained without power.[5] An economic system thus created a grave social problem. The socialist—and Communist—movements of the nineteenth century were the outcome of violent reaction to these desperate social conditions. Collective industrial labour and the poverty and injustice suffered by the whole working class led to a new solidarity among the workers, a solidarity which was quickly mobilized by the socialist movement in the "class war". After a long and bitter struggle, the capitalist economy and with it the power of capitalism were eventually broken, the *coup de grâce* being ultimately delivered after the great depression of 1929, which had repercussions throughout the world. The economic reforms based on the ideas of the English economist J. M. Keynes, which were introduced at about this

time, led to the "planned economy" which is now almost universally accepted.

The economic revolution has contributed more to the internationalization of relations in the world—including political relations—than any of the other revolutions discussed in this chapter. It is nowadays generally realized that prosperity can only be achieved if the dependence of nations on each other is clearly acknowledged and this mutual dependence is guaranteed by economic—and political—agreements and treaties. This social and economic revolution is, moreover, an event which has undeniably caused the course of human history to move in an entirely new direction.

Wars

I have given no more than a brief outline of these great revolutions. In my opinion, however, the important point to note is that, although their effects are different in each country, they have already taken place—no new revolutions have since occurred in the world. We have, however, experienced two major world wars. Wars are not in themselves revolutions, but the world wars of this century were conflicts in the sphere of international politics which came about as a result of obstructions in the path of the developments that were set in motion in the revolutions. One of these impediments was political nationalism. The scientific, the technical and industrial and the social and economic revolutions had made many existing institutions and current international policy out of date, but no adequate preparations had been made for the fundamental renewal of these institutions and this policy.

The First World War ended in a dubious compromise. Europe became much more open in its attitude and most of the surviving elements of feudalism were swept away, but the victorious powers discriminated against Germany and in so doing sowed the seeds of a fresh international conflict. Although it was widely recognized that no single nation could form an enclosed unit and the principle of internationalization was generally accepted in political and socio-economic relations in the world, nationalism appeared in a new form. Certain nations emerged, asserting supremacy over other nations. This tendency prevailed in Nazi Germany and Fascist Italy, who claimed leadership in Europe, and in Soviet Russia, who claimed world leadership.

The Second World War also ended in a compromise. The need for political, socio-economic and scientific unity and co-operation resulted in the setting up of the United Nations Organization and there was also an epoch-making expression of international idealism and humanitarian feeling in the Declaration of Human Rights. Colonialism was abolished in principle and a new feeling of responsibility towards the underdeveloped nations led to a world-wide attack on poverty in the form of international assistance. Enormous developments in the technological sphere have led to a great increase in communication and mobility and the principle of interdependence among the nations has become even more widely recognized. But, on the other hand, there has also been a sharp increase in tension between East and West since the Second World War and in thinking in terms of world powers striving for world domination. This has meant that we now live under the constant threat of a third world war, although, for the time being at least, our awareness of the consequences of the use of nuclear weapons has made this impossible. We have therefore reached a state of precarious balance in our international relations. This equilibrium must at all costs be maintained for as long as possible, to give us time to elaborate principles for the peaceful solution of these international conflicts.

Rapidation

These revolutions and the two world wars have resulted in the appearance of a number of entirely new phenomena which are of immense importance to the future of man and society. Among these new phenomena, I would mention the following—urbanization, or the tendency to live in ever larger urban agglomerations,[6] the continuous increase in world population, the possibility of measuring, calculating

44

and checking and of assimilating and automatically producing information and data in an entirely new way and with incredible speed (cybernetics and automation) and finally the enormous intensification of communications and the great expansion, to almost unlimited proportions, in mobility that has accompanied this increase in communications.

All these phenomena point to one basic factor—the increased speed of development in the world. And this brings me to what I regard as the essential aspect of our present situation and of the future.

Our situation is not, in my opinion, revolutionary. It is rather a situation that is characterized by a hitherto unknown acceleration in the course of events and by a growing estrangement from the traditional patterns of life and thought. Historical changes are taking place today with a speed that only a short time ago would have seemed incredible. These changes and developments are, however, not a revolution in the course of history, but an acceleration of historical events. That is why my first words in this book—in the introduction—were a reference to "rapid change" as the essential characteristic of our present age. This rapid change is an entirely new phenomenon of the mid-twentieth century and should not be confused with "revolution".

A new word has to be employed to denote a new phenomenon and I should like to use the word "rapidation" (and the adjective "rapidary") in this connection. I have chosen this word (although I agree that it is not beautiful), because it can mean "acceleration" or "speeding up". Sociologists, aware of the accelerated pace of developments today, often refer to "rapid change", although in a rather different context. Furthermore, the word "rapid" is used in several European languages to denote a sudden increase in speed in the current of, for example, a river ("rapids", *le rapide*, etc.) and this is perhaps the most appropriate image that can be found for the phenomenon that I have in mind.

The following definition can be supplied for this new phenomenon—*rapidation is a complex and comprehensive phenomenon of our present age in which an acceleration of*

45

historical developments takes place in all spheres of human
society in increasing discontinuity with the past.

The Unstable Character of Life

I shall not here go into the question of whether rapidation
is good or bad, or whether the accelerated pace of events
should be stimulated or checked. The important thing for us
to do now is to place on record that the phenomenon of
rapidation exists and to ask ourselves what it means for
the future. I am in fact convinced that we shall only be able
to say something meaningful about the future if we analyse
the phenomenon of rapidation and its consequences.

In the past, social, political and even ecclesiastical structures were much more static and enduring and the developments that took place in these structures were much more
gradual. It is quite obvious, however, that, because of rapidation, the world structures of today are far from static and
enduring. We are caught up in a rapid current of development, the end of which is not in sight. Indeed, we are bound
to wonder whether there is an end at all to this process of
rapid development. A great deal of the unrest that is felt
today, in the Church and outside it, stems from the fact that
powerful reactionaries have been clinging obstinately to
structures, and have been deeply entrenched in codifications,
which they believe are lasting and unchangeable and whose
relative and in fact already superseded character they refuse
to accept. Again, much of the deep anxiety and alarm that
is expressed today is due to the confusion caused by rapidation, to uncertainty about the form that the rapidly moving
world will eventually take. This fearful attitude has inevitably led to attempts to slow down or stem the tide of
developments in the modern world.

The traditional structures of society are beginning to break
down and crumble away. Many people are beginning to wonder if democracy in its traditional form can be preserved in
the future. The parliamentary system operates far too slowly
for decisions to be taken with the necessary speed. The problems which governments of today have to deal with are so

complicated that they cannot simply be put before, and explained to, parliaments, but have increasingly to be left to experts and special commissions if a country is not to be left behind in the process of rapidary development.

The consequences of rapidation were first felt and accepted in the sphere of business and commerce. Many modern businesses and industries were extremely reluctant to remain tied to fixed, permanent structures and patterns of work and management. Survival and success in the business and commercial world of today demand rapid adaptability to changes in a constantly moving market, great flexibility in the strategy and tactics of management, an ability to improvise quickly, an extremely subtle and almost intuitive sensitivity to fluctuations in supply and demand and a speedy reaction to all new developments. These industries have consequently set up special research departments which are constantly sounding new trends and examining new plans and adaptations of existing plans.

Modern business life is therefore more actively concerned with hypotheses, provisional tactics and flexible policies than with traditionally constituted norms of conduct and fixed patterns of working. The hypotheses are not given an absolute value and action based on existing hypotheses is preferred to waiting too long for possibly better hypotheses to be formulated. Faced with great fluidity in the existing situation, it is generally recognized that the need is for a flexible and hypothetical fabric of norms, policies and courses of action if a business or industry is to retain its vitality in the present and survive in the future.

I have devoted rather a lot of attention to this question because I believe that these developments in the sphere of business, commerce and industry are very much in tune with the real situation in the world today and throughout this whole discussion the Church has been constantly at the back of my mind. The Church too has a traditional structure and her functions have been codified according to certain current norms. My comparison between the Church and business life is, of course, imperfect, but there is nonetheless an important similarity between the two. The entire structure of the Church is faced with the phenomenon of rapidation and she dare not assume that she is above it. Precisely as a structure, the Church is incarnate in the world. But this structure and the Church's codifications, government, policy and guiding principles are derived from another age and a different situation. It will clearly become more and more difficult for the Church, because the phenomenon of rapidation means an increasing discontinuity with the past, to continue to make use of tradition and the experience of the past. These traditions and norms of the past are becoming less and less effective in determining the present and the future. They are not so much despised as regarded as no longer bearing, in themselves, the stamp of authenticity.[7]

It is therefore of the utmost importance that the Church should face up to the reality of the world of today if she is to have any future at all as a vital community.

I do not intend to go further into this question here. The problem will be discussed more fully in a later chapter.

Phenomena of Rapidation

It is important at this point to go a little more deeply into the phenomena to which reference has already been made earlier in this chapter—phenomena which have partly been instrumental in bringing about this process of rapidation and which have partly resulted from it.

1. *Urbanization.* By this I mean the constant expansion of urban civilization and the increasing growth of towns that is taking place in most parts of the world. Before the industrial revolution, a town or city was regarded as the centre of an independent human society, that is to say, it formed, together with the country that immediately surrounded it, a more or less self-contained whole. In our present civilization, this is no longer the case. Modern technology and means of transport and communication, the rise of the great industries, the population explosion and the constant and ever increasing flow of labour away from the land and em-

ployment in agriculture into industry and the various services in the towns have resulted in an enormous increase in urban population throughout the world. In an attempt to gain some insight into this phenomenon of urbanization, demographers and sociologists have adopted the following provisional definition of the urban or standard metropolitan area, namely, that it is an "urban unit with a population of at least 100,000, an agglomeration of a central town or of towns plus adjoining districts with economic links with this town and where 65% or more of the economically active population is employed in non-agricultural pursuits".[8] By urbanization, then, we mean the existence of an integrated system of urban centres or areas and interconnected districts, in which each part of the system makes its own special contribution to the division of labour within the whole. The whole in this case may be one country or a federation of countries.

Everything points to the fact that urbanization will continue to increase in the future. This does not necessarily mean, however, that more and more people will live in relatively small areas. On the contrary, continuing progress in the sphere of transport will certainly result in a centrifugal form of urbanization, so that the districts in which the inhabitants of these urban centres live will spread in ever widening circles around the original city centres. Indeed, when cheap transport, moving at the speed of sound (for example, in vacuum tunnels), becomes widely available, it will be quite possible for people to live as far as 120 miles or more away from their places of work.

There has also been, in the past, a distinct tendency towards keeping the areas in which people worked and those in which they lived to some extent apart. Certain residential areas were often referred to as "suburbs", but this term is rapidly becoming out of date. The suburbs, which have often been organized and administered as independent "towns", can, in the present rapidary tendency towards urbanization, no longer be effectively managed in this way, with the result that suburban "towns" are becoming more and more closely linked, in administration and government, to the so-called conurbation. In this way, the total urbanization of a metropolitan area can be administered and governed with a greater degree of co-ordination.

The town centre is the place where the business life, the official services, the municipal government, the cultural life and amusements (and often the industrial activities as well) of the town are concentrated. But even here there is a tendency towards centrifugal urbanization—the development, in large metropolitan areas, of several centres of this kind, closely linked to each other by modern means of communication. In such cases, it is possible to speak only of local decentralization.

The increasing industrialization and mechanization of agriculture and the increasing production of artificially manufactured foodstuffs will inevitably result in a continuing decline in the population of the rural areas and an even more rapid growth of urbanization. Sociologists are coming to see more and more clearly that the increase in world trade has played a very big part in the fact that urbanization has become a world phenomenon. Although the process of urbanization has to some extent decreased in the most urbanized parts of the world (in the United States and in North-West Europe, for example), it is constantly increasing in the underdeveloped countries and doing this at a steadily increasing tempo. The hinterland of the great towns of today is, in a word, the world itself—this is so because of the continued rapid growth of intercommunications and inter-relations between the great urban areas of the world. It is a frequent occurrence for enormous and mutually interconnected urban areas to arise within one single country. (The French sociologist, Jean Gottmann, has invented the term "megalopolis" for this phenomenon.) An example of this is the relatively narrow coastal strip of land along the eastern seaboard of the United States, between Boston and Washington, which is inhabited now by forty million people —almost a quarter of the total population of America

Urbanization does not, of course, only mean a quantitative

50

change in society—the concentration of a large number of people in relatively small areas. It has also resulted in a far-reaching change in the quality of society. This qualitative change has its light and its shadow. Urbanization has undoubtedly brought greater prosperity for many people and greater opportunities for the people to share in the cultural, social, artistic and scientific life of the country in which they live. But, on the other hand, there has also been a considerable increase in crime (especially juvenile crime), loneliness, depersonalization, neuroses, heart diseases, separation and divorce and political corruption, to name only a few of the darker sides of urbanization. The most urgent problem of urbanization, then, is how to live with it.

Finally, the great urban agglomerations have become areas of enormous political and economic power and influence It is in them that the most far-reaching decisions concerning the future of man and the world are taken. It is in them that the most important plans are formed for the progress or regress of mankind. And what is more, it is becoming increasingly clear that, because of the growing interconnection and interdependence of the great urban areas, no important decision can be confined to one single urban agglomeration or to one single country.[9]

I have discussed the phenomenon of urbanization in some detail because I am of the opinion that rapidation in this sphere presents mankind—even more than the other developments in modern society—with a challenge to revalue in a creative manner the existing social institutions. And this applies in particular to the Church institution.

2. *Increase in Population.* The phrase that is commonly used here is "population explosion". This term has much to recommend it, but it is not strictly correct, since an explosion is really a sudden and violent blowing up. The suggestive force of the word "explosion" in this context is, however, not out of place insofar as the rapidary increase in world population has assumed hitherto unknown proportions and has caused considerable alarm. United Nations

experts have estimated that the present world population will have doubled by the turn of the century.[10] Until the industrial revolution, the death rate due to disease, famine and wars was in most countries so high that it was barely exceeded by the birth rate. Since the industrial and social revolutions, however, the standard of living has increased enormously and the progress of medical science has caused the death rate to fall and the birth rate to rise. Between 1800 and 1950, the population of Europe increased from 187 to 559 million. In the same period, the population of the United States rose from 6 to 166 million. The populations of Asia and Africa, on the other hand, have "only" doubled in this time.

The first problem arising from this situation was that of inequality in opportunity and prosperity. Before the industrial revolution, the various countries of the civilized world differed little in their standard of living. Now, however, the poorest 54% of the world population (living in twelve countries) produces some 9% of the world's income, whereas the 7% of the world's population inhabiting the United States and Canada produces some 43% of the world's income. Formerly, the existence of very great economic differences between various countries was less important, mainly because poor communications made it difficult or impossible to compare one's standard of living with that of other countries and therefore to envy these other countries for their higher level of prosperity.[11] Now, however, this inequality between the richer countries of the West and the underdeveloped countries of the world is the greatest source of all political, social and economic unrest. Simple attempts to level out this inequality, by sending food and economic help, for example, to a starving country like India, contain an element of great danger. They may help to raise the standard of living slightly for a while, but they also bring about a lowering of the death rate, which in turn causes an increase in the population that is proportionately higher than the raised standard of living. The only result, then, is that the problem rapidly becomes even greater and gives rise to the question as to whether some form of population control should not accompany the sending of food and economic help to underdeveloped countries.

For the time being at least, the present rapidary increase in population will probably continue. It will also continue to be one of the great problems of the future. For it is a simple fact that the world population cannot go on increasing at the present rate. Even if the population of the world were to be more evenly distributed over the world's surface, every square yard of land that was capable of being cultivated would, in three hundred years' time, have to be made available for the production of food. But even if artificial human foodstuffs are successfully produced, the world will still be so full in two thousand years' time that there will be standing room only.[12]

It is therefore obvious that this is a problem that can no longer be solved by the methods that have hitherto been applied. It is also a problem which will face the Church in the very near future.

3. *Cybernetics (Automation, Computers)*.[13] The phenomenon that I wish to discuss in this section is so far without a universally accepted name. The current term in America, the continent of Europe and the Soviet Union is cybernetics. In England, however, it is frequently referred to as "control engineering" or "communication engineering". Sometimes the word "automation" is used for the whole phenomenon, although this word should only be applied, in the strictly technical sense, to machines which automatically yield products, whereas automatic calculating and thinking machines (computers) are quite different. I propose, for the sake of simplicity, to use the word "cybernetics" for all these various aspects of recent technical development.

The new theoretical and practical science of cybernetics (the word is derived from the Greek word for "steersman") evolved as a result of the need, in the Second World War, during which aircraft flying at ever greater speeds were developed, to develop at the same time more rapid and more accurate methods of reckoning and computing. An automatic "brain", capable of calculating more rapidly and with greater precision than the human brain, was urgently required. To this end, intensive scientific research was carried out by a group of logistic experts, mathematicians, electro-technicians and neurophysicists, led by Professor Norbert Wiener. This research rapidly produced astonishing results and Professor Wiener published his group's discoveries in a book which appeared in 1947, giving the new science the name of cybernetics.

The principles of cybernetics are very difficult, if not impossible, for the outsider to understand, but, at the risk of oversimplification, it can be said that this new science has enabled automatic machines to be designed which can assimilate and control a great amount of complex information and very many complex facts at incredible speed and even perform the most complicated calculations and draw logical conclusions in a very short space of time. It has also enabled various types of apparatus to be designed which can automatically carry out highly complicated tasks. The result is that we now have at our disposal machines which can think and machines which can do, and both these types of machine can, furthermore, be used in combination. Cybernetics, therefore, has made the following types of apparatus possible:

(*a*) apparatus for the automatic carrying out of complex tasks (for example, the automatic production of material objects and instruments);

(*b*) apparatus that can make complicated mathematical and logical calculations and can form conclusions (computers);

(*c*) apparatus that is a combination of (*a*) and (*b*), that is to say, computers which can, for example, work out an elaborate process of production by interpreting the data fed into them, coupled to other apparatus which can carry out the calculations made by these computers. Different types of cybernetic apparatus combined in this way can therefore calculate, regulate, control and carry out extremely complicated processes. Among these may, for example, be included the apparatus or combinations of apparatus which assimilate and deal with information and thereby provide man with the opportunity of understanding and regulating what takes place within a given environment.

These discoveries in the field of cybernetics are really sensational both because of the precision and the unparalleled speed with which they work and because of the many different uses to which they can be put. Indeed, they have almost unlimited possibilities. They can learn from experience, adapt themselves to various conditions and improve their performance on a basis of lessons learnt. They can reflect, deliberate and judge. They can even decide upon the best course of action under certain circumstances. It is even regarded as possible that they will eventually be able to reproduce themselves.

All this is bound to have enormously important consequences for the future of mankind. Professor Fred Polak has therefore formulated four laws in an attempt to clarify the future developments in the sphere of cybernetics:

1. These machines will continue to invade more and more new fields where man has hitherto held a monopoly as the only being endowed with reason.

2. In all these new spheres, previously regarded as specifically human, these machines will very quickly prove themselves superior to the human beings, with their limited faculties, whom they are imitating.

3. Among the known potential developments open to cybernetic machines at present, an increasingly large part will, in future, be played by those machines which are capable of making independent decisions.

4. In economic and social life of the future, more and more hitherto specifically or uniquely human forms of work will be taken over by such machines, which are superior in almost every respect.[14]

Although at first it gave rise to a good deal of derision, cybernetics is now taken very seriously. The advantages are many and undeniable. But there are also disadvantages, and these have caused a great deal of anxiety. The advantages

55

to business life are numerous—increase in the gross national product, cheaper and better methods of production, a more rational direction, a reduction in the number of tasks of management, the possibility of making more efficient decisions and the simplification of complex administration. The government of a country can be based on speedy and precise information. Professor Polak is extremely optimistic and believes that cybernetics will make for better international relationships in the future and will render a third world war impossible.

But there is also the other side of the coin. Cybernetics will undoubtedly result in a great deal of unemployment, especially among the untrained and semi-trained workers. For the time being at least, only unsatisfactory solutions have been suggested. At first it was believed that the surplus workers could be transferred to the administrative and service branches of society, but it soon became clear that automation would also cause unemployment in that sector as well. The most satisfactory solution that has been suggested up to the present is a drastic limitation of hours of work. But this gives rise to a fresh problem—the employment of free time. For the great majority of unskilled and less gifted people, too much free time may well lead to boredom and frustration on a large scale, and this in turn may lead to social unrest and aggression.

Finally, the wide application of automation contains another grave danger for man in the future. Cybernetic machinery is so useful to man in the mass that the planning offices will, as Donald Michael has observed, be tempted to develop a society with aims that can be achieved more easily in terms of the mass than in terms of the individual. The generally accepted use of computers gives rise to the danger that attention will be principally directed towards those aspects of reality which can be fed into and assimilated by a computer, with the result that cybernetics may develop into an attempt to eliminate what is individual and variable in man.[15]

Norbert Wiener's warning in this connection deserves to be

taken very seriously: "Whether we entrust our decisions to machines or to offices, great laboratories, armies and enterprises . . . we shall never get a correct answer to our questions unless we ask the right questions".[16] And here, such questions arise as, what do we really want to achieve? what is man? what is the ultimate aim of man and of mankind? These are questions which even the most highly developed computer cannot answer. But they are questions which will confront us more and more in the cybernetic world of the future.

4. *Economic and social internationalization as a result of growing interdependence.* In a speech on Independence Day, 4 July 1962, the late President Kennedy made a "declaration of interdependence", a play of words on the "declaration of independence". This declaration was criticized by certain American politicians, but it accurately reflected the great change that has taken place in the world since 1950. Since the development in Western Europe of a third economic giant (to use Adlai Stevenson's phrase), it has no longer been possible to think in terms of two great political and economic giants in the world, America and Russia. The Treaty of Rome, concluded in 1957, has brought into being the European Economic Community which, as far as population (170 million people) and resources are concerned, is almost equal to the United States or Soviet Russia. Within the Common Market, economic development is so "rapidary" that production is expected to equal that of the United States by 1975. In addition, other countries and federations of countries have also become economically more important and influential, and various economic relationships have automatically come about between these countries and groups of countries and attempts have subsequently been made to stabilize and safeguard these relationships by political means.

Thus, in a very short space of time, economic, political and even social relationships have come about between many different countries in all parts of the world, and these relationships have been strengthened by a concentration of forces in the sphere of technical and scientific research. Shortly after the Second World War, Karl Jaspers was able to write that mankind already formed a unity which was "founded on the fact that nothing important can happen anywhere which does not affect everyone".[17] A well-known economist, who is at the same time also a sociologist, has referred to the entirely new aspect of this interdependence and to the fact that it is all-embracing.

> Modern man lives in a situation of dynamism with his neighbour which has never existed before to such an extent. This situation, involving a relationship between men and social complexes living in immediate contact with each other and therefore dependent on each other, has already extended to the whole of mankind. This means that, from now onwards, men can only live or die, prosper or suffer economically, *together*. There is no longer any possibility of national or regional monopolies in power or prosperity continuing to exist independently. In this sense, we are confronted with a process of fundamental democratization in international relationships.[18]

The phenomenon of the welfare state only appears to point to the possibility of a monopoly. In fact, the existence of underdeveloped, non-welfare states is a source of unrest and political and economic tension. A certain minimum welfare throughout the whole world is clearly something towards which we must aim in the future.

This, of course, gives rise to many serious questions, such as, for example, the question as to whether the satisfaction of the individual's needs and the creation of a welfare state will automatically lead to peace and social harmony.[19] It would be impossible to go into this and related questions here, but one great possibility which is implied in this phenomenon of world-wide interdependence of human relations, that of a political, social and economic internationalization and unification of the world, may be briefly discussed. Will it in fact be possible to develop a political, social and economic superstructure on a world-wide scale which can act as a "world government" in the service of human progress.? And would such a world government be able to bring about the unity of the world and yet preserve regional and national differences? Is this simply a distant utopian dream, or is it something which can be achieved, in a period of rapidation, in the near future? If these questions can be answered in the affirmative, then the age-old dream of the unity of mankind will be realized. But this unity, for which Christianity and the Church consciously strove in the past, will be a secularized unity.

5. *Communication and Mobility.* Communication and mobility are really a direct consequence of the four phenomena that I have already discussed in the preceding paragraphs. In a complicated urban society with a rapidary increase in population and interdependent relationships, they are simply the result of a situational necessity.

By "communication", I do not simply mean *means* of communication, such as motor transport, aircraft, newspapers, books, television, radio and the telephone. In the first place, I mean the possibility of communicating with one's fellow men, of making oneself understood and of exchanging meaningful experiences. This has always taken place, mainly through the medium of language, but also by means of gestures, rites, symbols and actions. Communication is, however, not something that takes place in one direction. A definite "response" has always been aimed at, and this response forms an integral part of all communication.

What is new about communication today is the apparently boundless and rapid manner in which language, gesture, image and action can be multiplied. An image, a gesture and a word can, for example, be reproduced in a moment on thirty million television screens. Knowledge of disasters, political events and sensational developments can thus become the common property of all mankind in very little time. Modern techniques of reproduction have made the cultural achievements of the present and the past and technical and scientific developments of the present age rapidly available to the masses. In business and commercial life, rapid communication has become an imperative demand. This worldwide communication does, however, mean that a certain degree of communal understanding is necessary if any intelligible intercommunication is to take place. International contacts are still subject to a great number of difficulties—the interchange of ideas between men of different cultural and ideological backgrounds is frequently not only barely possible, but even entirely out of the question. In the future, however, intercommunication on a global scale is regarded as something which can certainly be achieved, and optimistic sociologists are of the opinion that it will result in lasting world peace.

But this all-embracing intercommunication also has many disturbing disadvantages. Large bodies, such as industrial organizations and even more particularly the state, are glad to make use of these means of communication for propaganda purposes and tend to employ them to mould men's minds. Vance Packard, in *The Hidden Persuaders* and the *Image Makers*, and other writers have shown clearly how easy it is to manipulate the human mind, so that communication can lead to a new kind of slavery of the spirit. What is more, it is frequently asserted that modern means of communication only bring about a superficial exchange of ideas and that the deeper dimensions of the human mind have become less communicable and more cut off than ever before.

Increased communication between men is accompanied by greater mobility. In static civilizations, man was tied geographically to his immediate surroundings. The great number and great variety of fast modern vehicles have meant that man is now extremely mobile and far less tied than in the past to a fixed locality. Industrialization and urbanization are developments which have resulted in modern man's extreme mobility. World society has made it technically possible for man to be easily and quickly transferred from one place to another. Now this rapid transferability is an economic necessity. Certain authors, especially sociologists, have referred to the dangers of this increased and accelerated mobility, the chief danger, in their opinion, being that modern man has been deprived of his roots. It is open to doubt whether the modern phenomenon of human mobility need be interpreted so negatively. The fact remains, however, that it will certainly develop even further in the future.

Some Conclusions

I shall no doubt be criticized for having left out of my list of five points various other aspects of modern society which are instrumental in determining the future. This may, of course, be true. I was not aiming to present a complete picture, but simply to provide a few important pointers to future developments within our present-day situation—a situation which is often so difficult to see as a whole.

When the situation is viewed as a whole, then in my opinion one thought emerges from all the developments that I have attempted to outline as predominant—the idea that man himself is autonomous and responsible for himself, for the world and for the future of mankind. It would be entirely wrong to see the course of events in the world as caused by blind fate, by divine providence or by some mindless process of nature. It is man himself who fashions the human world and is responsible for the course of history.

This chapter has gradually become a continuation of the previous chapter, in which I was concerned to find the reason for the question mark which follows everything that we say about the future of the Church. In the first chapter, we looked at this problem from inside. Within a Christianity that is constantly becoming less relevant, a struggle has developed—a struggle to solve the problems of secularization and inadequate proclamation of the Christian message. Both these problems go back ultimately to a failure on the part of the Church.

In this second chapter, we have looked at the situation from outside—from the point of view of the world. At first sight, the problem within the Church and the problem outside Christianity would seem to have little in common.

Nonetheless, there is a connection between the two. The Church has only recently discovered the real extent of secularization and it was an extremely painful discovery. Then, at the Council, the Church gave the first sign that she openly recognized this problem in Schema 13, and especially in that part of the schema which deals with the Church and society. It is possible that, in using a term like "cultural metamorphosis" (par. 4) to describe the situation, the Church is revealing her awareness of the phenomenon of rapidation. But the Council's formulations were, in part at least, rather vague and were, moreover, attempts to catch up with developments that had already taken place. Nonetheless, it was clearly realized that secularization was moving towards a worldly autonomy with regard to man's destiny and the future of society (par. 55). The Church is well aware of the dangers inherent in this kind of autonomy, especially if man becomes self-sufficient through complete trust in the progress of science and technical ability (par. 69).

But how is the Church to have any influence on modern, secular society? This question did not receive a clear answer in the Council. The difficulty here is that the decrees and constitutions of the Council certainly provide visions, but are rather vague about how these things can be worked out within the present structure of the Church.

Modern man feels that he is autonomous and responsible in connection with the problems of urbanization, increasing population, cybernation, social and economic internationalization and global intercommunication and he has faith in his technical and scientific ability to solve these problems of man and society. Surely the Church cannot hope to have any influence on the vision of modern, secular man simply by making declarations and issuing a number of publications? We have never come any closer to peace in the world simply by hearing the Pope speak messages of good will at Christmas.

Somewhere there is a short circuit, and it is our task to trace this. Are there perhaps heretical structures in the Church which are frustrating the Church's message and her mission even more effectively than dogmatic heresies?[20] Or is the Church prevented by her present structure, as an independent institution with its own prestige, from being *present* in precisely those places where secular man is seeking and asking questions, planning and creating? This is the question which we now have to try to answer.

III

The Church in the Secular Situation

The Church will have to simplify her pattern of life radically in the future. KARL RAHNER.[1]

A. SEEN FROM THE POINT OF VIEW OF THE CHURCH

THE presence of the Church in the world of today and to-morrow—the questions which rise in this connection are so many and so urgent that we can hardly continue to by-pass the fundamental question, What do we really mean by the "Church"? I intend to go more deeply into this in a later chapter; in the meantime, however, it is necessary to give a very brief outline of what is meant by "Church" here. I propose in the first place to give an abstract and ideal description of the Church, then to correct this description by referring to the Church's actual mode of existence and finally to provide a view of the Church as she is seen by an outsider.

The Church is both an event and an institution, in which men are called together and united to each other by a common faith in Christ and his message. Those who have been called together in this way know that Christ bestows healing and redeeming power on mankind, which suffers from a certain impotence with regard to its real destiny. Thus, in the person of Jesus of Nazareth, the real meaning of human existence is made public and, within this revelation, the mystery of God himself is made public as a nearness in love. The Church experiences her unity with Christ and the unity of her members by a sharing in the eucharistic meal. The Church is, however, not a closed circle, realizing and expressing the salvation brought by Christ only within her own walls. She also has the task of manifesting the life of Christ in and to this world. For this reason, she has two basic structures—the structure of proclamation and that of being a sign (sacrament).[2] Both these structures presuppose that she is visible and present in the world. The proclamation (which includes far more than simply preaching) means that the saving event of the past is relevant to the present and the future. Her primary sacramental character is realized by the Church's being an effective sign of the "life in Christ" for the salvation of the world.

Everything that has been said about the Church so far can be applied to the local as well as to the universal Church. The unity of the local church with all other local churches in one whole is above all the function of the hierarchical office. At the head of a local church is the parish priest, who is in turn dependent on and associated with the larger local church—the diocese. At the head of the dioceses are the bishops, who are in their turn *in communio* with each other as a college. The one Church therefore consists of many local churches communicating with each other. The network of communions that the Church forms in this way has its nodal points in the bishops. Finally, there is in the Catholic Church one decisive point of orientation in this unity of communion—the bishop of Rome.[3]

Taking it as a whole, this is, of course, rather an abstract and even ideal definition of the Church. In the course of history, there have been developments which have led to the original unity of the Church—a unity of heart and soul, of eucharistic communion and joint confession of faith—undergoing a shift of emphasis and becoming more of an institutional, juridical and administrative unity. The strength of the Church's unity has gradually come to be situated more and more in organized uniformity and centralization. More and more faith was placed in a canonically *organized* unity, which was expressed above all in a high degree of uniform thought in theology and in uniform moral precepts and liturgical regulations, all controlled and directed centrally from the Church's central authority in Rome. (The Council brought about a strong counter-movement in connection with these developments.)

To the outsider, the Roman Catholic Church therefore appears as a tightly organized and centrally controlled religious institution with its own distinctive authority and prestige. Within the Church, there is a clear polarity between laity and clergy. The clergy obviously occupies a privileged position, not only because the Church's priests administer the word and the sacraments, but also because they are entrusted with almost every authoritative function in the Church. They seem to be in almost exclusive charge of the "missionary task" or apostolate. The aim of this apostolate, which has various means at its disposal, is to keep the membership of the Church constant and if possible to increase it. The Church also attempts to influence certain secular structures by setting up organizations and associations of her own. Finally, she is territorially organized, that is to say, she has accurately defined regions of power (dioceses) within which a bishop exerts a spiritual and canonical authority. These regions are in turn divided into smaller territories (parishes), each with a parish priest in charge.

This close and complex degree of organization is undoubtedly one of the most impressive aspects of the Catholic Church for the outsider.

Alienation and Absence

If we now ask once again the question that we asked at the beginning of this chapter—Is the Church present in the world?—we may say that the Church certainly makes a powerful impression as an institution at least and that secular man cannot, in this sense, deny her existence.

But this is not the point at issue. Being present in the world is not simply a question of passively or even impressively "being there". It is a question of being really involved in the situation of here and now. The Church must be a manifestation of the "life in Christ". She must proclaim the message of the gospel and she must do this in the very heart of our modern society. In my opinion, the Church is not present in this sense, and the logical conclusion to be drawn from this is that, if the Church continues to do what she is now doing and to be what she is now, then she has no future. Her fine churches and beautiful cathedrals will become the sepulchral monuments, the graves of God and of Christianity.

We must above all be alive to the real, existing situation, and this is perhaps that the Church, because of her inadequate proclamation of the Christian message and possibly most of all because of her present structure, is becoming more and more irrelevant to our modern secular society. If the Church continues simply to embroider on her traditional pattern, then her testimony just *cannot* be really heard any more.

The reason for this is that the Church has—apparently—sought refuge, structurally, in the purely private sphere of life and, what is more, has come to feel completely at home there as well. She has become alienated, if not completely absent, from the creative and dynamic centres of society. In those very spheres in which man gives thought to, and plans and realizes, his world and the world of the future and his possibilities and those of the human race, the Church and her testimony are clearly absent.[4]

This has not always been the case. In the Middle Ages, Church and society were to some extent identical. The priority of the spiritual kingdom was recognized and this resulted in the supreme authority in medieval society being attributed to the Church (although this caused frequent conflicts in the course of history). Nonetheless, the Church was, through the medium of her clergy, always effectively present in society at this time. With the Reformation, however, this pattern was broken and the Church withdrew into her own enclave and became a clearly defined institution existing alongside human society, despite her constant attempts, throughout the Counter-Reformation, to restore the myth of European unity in the face of the emerging powers of the new world. The Church was driven back more and more within her own doors—but she also voluntarily withdrew herself within these doors. In this way, she developed the structure of an institution existing *alongside* the structures of public society.

If it is true, then, that the Church has, over the centuries, ceased to be part of the creative and centrally dynamic structures of society, then we are faced with the question of where the Church is in fact present now. In the first place, she is clearly present in her clergy. This is, however, both traditionally and structurally, a closed circle. Celibacy alone has made the Church's clergy a relatively enclosed environment, and attempts to "open" this environment a little more have led at once to problems in connection with the celibacy of the priesthood. The worker-priest movement was bound to fail for this reason alone. The present crisis in the Catholic priesthood is a result of the experience of many priests that the closed environment of the priesthood must be broken, but that there are as yet no suitable structures which would make this break-through possible.

But this clerical sphere is of the greatest importance in the dialogue between the Church and the world. It is, after all, within this sphere that the Church's thought, leadership and decisions take place. But the fact that this sphere is so cut off and self-enclosed (and the clergy becomes increasingly cut off from the world the higher one goes up the hierarchical ladder) is a very great handicap to the Church's creative presence in society. In a word, the Church cannot be effectively and significantly present in the structures of modern society because of her clergy.

The Church in the Residential Environment

But the Church is also clearly and emphatically present in another sphere—because of her parochial system, she is present in the residential environment. But it is already becoming clear that this is not without its problems. The cultural and social units on which the parish system had traditionally been based are disappearing in an age of increasing urbanization. The centres of most of our cities and towns are becoming depopulated and are being given over almost entirely to business and industrial life. Some old established parishes in the city centres linger on, but many of them have lost almost all their parishioners and the churches have been closed. In the fringe areas of our towns, however, new residential agglomerations have sprung up with incredible speed and these are scarcely covered by the parochial system. The division between the residential and the working sectors of our towns is thus becoming increasingly obvious. The most recent parochial developments are concentrated in these new districts, which generally consist of fairly arbitrarily defined residential agglomerations. Imperceptibly, the Church has—even in the physical sense—left the creative and dynamic heart of society, for this heart is hardly beating at all in the residential districts. History is made and man is creatively planning his future not in the residential zones on the fringes of our towns, but in the central spheres of science and technology, of politics and economics, of controlled urbanization, of industry and production and of planning, accounts and finance.

Many Catholics refuse to recognize the extent to which the Church has become alienated from these central structures of society. They have, of course, seen that the Church was absent from these secular structures, but they have convinced themselves that it was possible to solve the problems by continuing to work with the basic structure of the Church developed since the Reformation and by setting up parallel structures, generally under the guidance of the clergy. (Examples of these, particularly in Europe, have been the Catholic political parties, the Catholic trade union and professional organizations and so on.) None of this has, however, been an effective presence within the creative centres of our society. It has only been a setting up of parallel institutions *alongside* these creative centres.

We can say, then, that the Church is visibly and effectively present in the modern residential agglomerations. Geographically speaking, these are the places where an emotionally stable family life is ideal. They are the enclaves where people can find refuge and a certain peace, where they can lick their wounds and devote themselves to the bringing up of their children. It is undeniably important that the Church should be present, in her proclamation of the message and her witness to the faith, in this residential and family environment. But it should not be forgotten that this sphere is only one of the many sectors within the vast pattern of contemporary society. It is in these residential districts that people look for peace and security alongside the world, for a therapeutic counterbalance to the tensions caused by life in the dynamic centres of the public sector

In these residential environments, the Church is above all concerned with the task of involving people, as far as possible, in a community of Sunday worship. Although the celebration of the Eucharist is undoubtedly important and indeed essential, the way in which it takes place does not guarantee that the Christian consciousness will be made more intensely present and bear a more intense witness in the macrostructure of our modern society. Even since the liturgical renewal resulting from the Second Vatican Council and the great impetus which this has given to the full and active participation of all Christians in the Mass, the celebration of the Eucharist still remains, *in fact*, far too much of a religious "practice" within the enclosed and private sphere. And because this "practice" is obligatory, it is still unconsciously experienced as something legalistic. The Catholic still "fulfils his Sunday obligation" and this fulfilling of a duty to the Church still gives the Catholic the satisfaction that he has proved and confirmed his belonging to the Church to himself and to other people. Of course, many faithful experience the Mass in a deeply religious manner as a becoming-one with the Lord and probably also as a sign of mutual love. But we also know from experience that for many the Mass is partly a religious, partly a conventional matter.

In any case, the actual manner of celebrating the Eucharist today is neither suited nor sufficient to make Christians really aware of their task in the very centre of modern society. What we have, then, is a *Christianity of the private sphere*, which has very little to do with the reality of everyday life. Those Christians whose actions on Monday disprove what they have confessed with their lips on Sunday are, alas, only too well known.

It is, however, said that all these practising Christians are nonetheless strengthened in their faith on Sunday and can be present as witnesses in all these different spheres of society precisely because of this faith. But this is simply an impressive theory which falls to pieces when confronted with the facts. In practice, every layman simply has to try to manage on his own to give form and content to his Christianity and to make his faith effective in the concrete, but often extremely difficult, circumstances, relationships and problems which face him in his day to day activities, judgments and decisions. He is left to his own devices in all his association with and in every aspect of his dealings with the "powers" of work, money, politics, technology, production, advertising, welfare and so on, and must do without the support and encouragement of his fellow Christians who are in the same position as he is and without the help of the proclamation of the Christian message which is nonetheless put to the test in his particular problem.[5]

In the residential environment of the parish, where the Church is quite emphatically present and has a distinctive and visible form, the Church's most important activity is probably Sunday worship. The parish priest has succeeded when he has managed to get as many people as possible from his parochial area to church on Sunday. In addition to the administration of the other sacraments, pastoral care consists also of a proclamation of the Christian message which often concentrates exclusively on individual and private values. These days, parishioners are frequently encouraged to join actively in the liturgy, but the liturgical texts themselves are often obscure because they are derived from outdated Church practice (the whole mystique of baptism in Lent and Easter is an example of this) and because the frequently mythological phraseology makes a real understanding of the liturgy difficult. Preachers readily lapse into pseudo-religious sentimentality or tend to moralize, exhorting the faithful to keep to the moral precepts of the Church or emphasizing the need to encourage the growth of the purely personal spiritual life. I do not deny that the situation is quite different in some churches, but I wish to stress that it is important to take as our starting-point not an ideal situation, but the situation as it exists widely in fact. Any priest who has spent long hours in the confessional knows that the conscience of the average Catholic has been formed almost exclusively in accordance with a Christian (?) morality which is almost entirely confined to the private sphere of life.

I am not maintaining that all the things that I have listed above are entirely without value, but I do think that it is difficult to dispute the inadequate character of a Church life that is manifested principally in a more or less enclosed form of worship and that lays stress on an unworldly liturgical piety, on individual morality and on pietistic values. One cannot help wondering where a Church life of this kind ties up with the macrostructure of modern society. Is the Church simply there in order to unite her members, on a basis of her traditional structures, in a self-enclosed celebration of the Eucharist and to provide them with peace, trust, pious feelings, a certain spiritual balance and a prospect of eternal life?

Professor Gibson Winter has commented succinctly on the whole problem: "A ministry to individuals and families in the context of residential association is no longer a ministry to society—in mass society, individuals contribute to decisions for the good or ill of the society, but they make these contributions through the managerial hierarchies, labour unions, community organizations, political bodies and bureaucratic units which organize their lives."[6]

Urbanization has resulted in an ever widening gulf between man's private life and his public existence. The Church tends to concentrate, in this situation, on man's needs in the private sphere and, in my opinion, there is something wrong with the Church's apparently unperturbed withdrawal into this circumscribed and restricted sphere of life. I believe that the Church has been called, in the gospel, to be a city set on a hill that cannot be hidden, a lamp put, not under a bushel, but on a stand so that everyone can see it and profit from it. It is therefore disturbing to witness the

Church's avoidance, up to the present, of all encounter with the powers which control the public life of modern secular and urban man. She is apparently powerless to exert any real influence on the course that urbanization is taking because she is not herself present within the forces which are determining the world of the future. Urbanization, growing world population, cybernetics, internationalization and world-wide communication and mobility are secular structures and developments which go to the very roots of human existence. Never before in human history has man had such an opportunity to control his own destiny, give scope to his own possibilities, determine the direction of his own development and plan his future on such a massive and world-wide scale. And yet it is quite clear that the Church and Christianity have, precisely at this momentous period of history, even less influence within this situation, and I have suggested that the cause of this decreasing influence is the present structure of the Church herself.

This is, however, not an entirely correct assessment of the situation, because it is obvious that modern society does not really welcome any serious influence on the part of the Church or religion in the public sphere. The complete division between Church and State is regarded as the most ideal situation in a modern democratic State. Any guardianship or indeed any say at all in the running of industry or in the sphere of production, science, technology, planning and so on, on the part of the churches or of religion generally, is regarded as somehow absurd. On the other hand, it is obvious that modern industrial and urban society is bound to assign the care and preservation of the personal, individual and private lives of men and their relationships with each other within the private sphere to the churches and to religion. It is important for us to recognize the existence of this aspect of the problem as well if we are to be completely honest and to view the situation as a whole.

B. THE OTHER SIDE OF THE PROBLEM

Before the social, technical and industrial revolutions,

The Grave of God

Christianity was *the* religion of Western civilization of the time and, before the Reformation, the Church was even a social superstructure which dominated the whole pattern of society. With the emergence of the modern pattern of society, there was a gradual emancipation from all religious and ecclesiastical ties, resulting eventually in the complete secularization of social relationships.

The philosopher Hegel, who lived during the period of transition from the older pattern of society to the new industrial society, saw this tendency towards secularization above all as a growth towards a society which was based principally on the *satisfaction of human needs.* All other forces and structures, such as religion, the churches and cultural and national traditions, which had previously determined society were relegated to the sphere of personal and individual freedom. In contrast to earlier social systems, society was at this time confined to those social relationships which joined individual men together in the satisfaction of their material needs through collective work.[7]

Hegel foresaw, then, the emergence of an age of universal conformity, levelling out of society on a massive scale. But, unlike so many contemporary critics of society, he was aware of the dialectic antipole of the situation. In his view, the objectivization, the matter-of-fact character and the functional nature of modern social relationships were bound to result in the emergence of a new and free sector in society, the private sector, within which man could, more than ever before, lead his own personal and individual life.[8] The social pressure of religion, Church, nationality and civilization was bound to become less, and man would be valued in modern society *as man* because he was a man and not because he was a Jew, a Catholic or a Protestant, a German or an Italian.[9]

A well-known contemporary sociologist has written:

The conformity of modern society and its tendency to level out has made an unprecedented number and variety of tastes, values and opinions available to the individual.

74

As a result of this, a very great and varied number of informal groupings runs across the large social organizations that are becoming increasingly uniform. In this way, the age of new bureaucratic uniformity is at the same time a historical period in which a unique unfolding of personal and intellectual life is taking place.[10]

H. Schelsky has come to more or less the same conclusion: "Conformity and individualization both have their origin in the fact that social relationships are becoming looser and less stringent. . . . The mobility of industrial society is, on the one hand, making adaptation to conforming social patterns easier and, on the other, favouring the preservation of the private and personal sphere."[11]

Many pessimists are in the habit of claiming that only bad results, such as an "anonymous existence", the "loss of identity", loneliness and depersonalization, can come of modern society, but this is a very one-sided view, which ignores the new freedom that has come about in the personal sector of human life.

Harvey Cox has seen this very clearly. He maintains that it would be impossible to enjoy personal, intimate relationships with everyone in an urban society in which such great numbers of people live cheek by jowl. In the public sector of life in the great urban communities, most human relationships *have to be* impersonal and matter-of-fact. If all human relationships within businesses, industries and services were intimate personal relationships, modern society would simply collapse. In the public sphere, therefore, modern man has to keep conforming, matter-of-fact relationships and patterns of life. On the other hand, however, he is even freer in his private life. Urban society provides him with a free—and a greater and wider—choice in many different spheres (for example, in his choice of schools, professions, clubs, friends, partners in marriage, theatrical entertainment and artistic expression). Cox therefore concludes: "Urban man . . . wants to maintain a clear distinction between private and public. Otherwise public life would overwhelm and dehumanize him."[12]

The Grave of God

The division between the public and the private sectors in modern society is also quite visible locally in urbanization, where the boundaries between the working areas and the residential areas are becoming more and more clearly defined. This division between work and private life has, of course, caused a certain tension, if not a cleavage, in the life of modern man. His most important task is to live meaningfully and in a state of balance within the tension that exists between his public and his private life and the entirely different parts which he has to play in these spheres.

The Place of Culture and Religion

One great difficulty in modern society is to give a meaningful place in life to religion and culture. Those members of society whose personalities are more developed tend to take up one or other aspect of culture as a leisure-time interest or pursuit. On the other hand, however, those who are less developed or less gifted tend to be the easy victims of the superficial sensations provided by an amusement industry which cashes in on the need which so many people, who experience a deep frustration in a matter-of-fact, unadventurous and impersonal society, feel for sensation and excitement. There is so much more free time available nowadays for the private sector of life and it has to be whiled away somehow—an indication that our newly gained freedom is not an unmixed blessing.

Religion and the Church are in a similar situation. Religion is no longer a public and social obligation, but a private affair. The Church tends to concentrate mainly on a spirituality of the "interior life", in other words, an individual spirituality and personal piety. This is combined with an emphasis on individual morality that specializes in human relationships in the private sphere, and one consequence of this is that the ethics of marriage and the family are particularly stressed nowadays. Indeed, it would seem that the morality of marriage constitutes the Church's greatest ethical problem of this century. Christian love is understood and is given form within the sphere of private encounters between fellow

76

human beings, but is not applied in any way to the sphere of political justice or to the whole field covered by the social macrostructures.

This development is fully in accordance with what modern society expects of the Church and religion. The Church is expected to see to it that a healthy situation prevails in the private sphere of life. Through the medium of her apostolate of industry, the Church is permitted to enter the field of modern industrial life, but only in order to create "better human relationships". These do, after all, improve the effectiveness of collective labour and consequently increase production. This is a remarkable case of Christian love serving industrial production. But the Church is not permitted to intervene in any way when, for example, the aim of this production is the total elimination of a competitor in the same field, by the creation of a monopoly of power, or when it is concerned with the manufacture of munitions or implements of war.

There are theological schools which emphasize this deep cleavage between public and private ethical activity. The usual point of departure for this theology is that the public structures of industry, business life, economics, technology and politics are (evil) "powers" which have to be resisted by a turning inwards into personal subjectivity. According to this theology, then, faith is based above all on personal subjectivity and is determined by "decisions" and "encounters" and not by the public patterns of society or the autonomous rationality of the industrial, economic, technical or political structures.

This is the general direction taken by the Protestant theological school of Rudolf Bultmann (a theologian who has incidentally also had a considerable influence on many Catholic theologians). According to this school, faith is the "total reflection of man about himself"[13] and is, in Bultmann's well-known phrase, a question of the human subject's "understanding of himself". Faith is man's reception of himself from God's hands, by which man is situated in a radical solitude, but is free "to go consoled through the darkness

77

and mysteries and to take on and bear the responsibility for the *act* in the solitude of his own decision."[14] This "act", however, only relates to man's private existence, which also includes encounters between fellow human beings. Like Robinson, Bultmann also interprets the parable of the sheep and the goats (Matt. 25. 31-46) as the appearance of God, *incognito*, on the level of private fellow-humanity.[15] Unfortunately, he does not take into consideration the fact that hunger, thirst and nakedness can also be involved in social structures. Gerhard Ebeling has also expressed more or less the same idea: "The Church is not an involvement with the abstract individual, but with man in his fellow-humanity."[16]

This does provide a partial solution to the enigma of the churches' inadequate proclamation of the message in a secular society (see Chapter I). In the course of these historical developments, the Church has been gradually and imperceptibly forced back into the sphere of the personal and private life of the individual. This has meant that her field of activity has become severely limited and that any attempt on her part to influence the public sector of society strikes us as strange and absurd and even as a usurpation of power.

I hasten to add, however, that what I have said so far does not mean that I should welcome a return to the medieval situation in which the Church, as a *cultus publicus* and an all-embracing *corpus christianorum*, permeated the whole fabric of society. "We must rid ourselves once and for all of the idea that somehow or other Western civilization has got to be or can be 're-Christianized' through some restoration, in a new guise, of the *Corpus Christianum*."[17]

The Hidden Threat

The vague feeling of uneasiness that we have today is due to our having become aware of the fact that the Church has completely lost touch with the public sphere of society. This awareness is in turn the result of our observation that the sharp division between the private and the public sectors of human life is not absolute, but perhaps even illusory. It is true that the structures are separate, but the influence of the public sector of contemporary society on the private sector is increasing alarmingly.

What is remarkable is that the public sector of life, as manifested in the whole of the technical and industrial and social and economic suprastructure of our society, has no clearly defined ideology (unlike that of the Communist society). This does not mean, however, that there is no dominating ideology (and I emphasize dominating) within our social structures.

This prevailing ideology consists of a great number of convictions which are often not expressed but simply taken for granted. They might be called the pseudo-myths of our society. In themselves, they are not regarded as problematical and are therefore very rarely questioned. In order to make the matter at issue clear, I should like to list a number of these generally accepted convictions, but in this connection it should be noted that each one, taken on its own, is open to criticism as a rather crude generalization. This is, of course, because the ideology of our Western society is not officially formulated, not systematized, and has a somewhat hidden character. Furthermore, these pseudo-myths vary from country to country.

What we have to do with, then, are assumptions which are difficult to pin down and to a great extent unconscious, such as:

With the help of work, science and technology, mankind makes progress;

progress is greater welfare;

welfare is the consequence of satisfying our material needs;

man's spiritual needs (culture and religion) must be looked after in the private sector of society;

everything that cannot be looked after in the private sector and therefore threatens the smooth running of affairs in the public sector must be taken out of the hands of private initiative;

time is money;

money is power;

79

success (financial, political or in one's career) means happiness;

the best paid job is the best job;

you must succeed in life, it doesn't matter how;

all uncertainties must be eliminated;

only useful things are good;

too much speculation can be dangerous;

our social system is good;

everything must be so arranged that it can be regulated and controlled;

anything that cannot be measured or calculated is valueless;

all radical criticism of society must be suppressed;

questions that cannot be answered must be avoided;

you must keep the people happy by providing plenty of food and recreation;

people who don't fit into our society are anti-social or inferior;

the individual and variable elements in man must be reduced to a minimum;

reality is identical with what is empirically verifiable;

what cannot be discussed (the ineffable, the mysterious, the symbolical) must not be discussed.

It would of course be possible to extend this rather arbitrary list indefinitely. In any case, it would be interesting to make a conscious ideology of these hidden and unquestioned assumptions that are taken for granted in the public sector of our society.

Of course, there are people who see through this ideological background to our life today, but they are only relatively few in number and are powerless as individuals to do anything about it. All these assumptions are accepted by the great majority of people as a normal climate in which to live. From time to time there is a mass reaction against certain measures, such as unemployment, restrictions in spending and price and tax increases, which are regarded as severely limiting human freedom. But most people resign themselves quickly enough to such new situations, because the machinery of the public sector is, in the last resort, always anonymous and its ideology is always hidden and unknown. This is the great strength of the social ideology of the Western world today—it is anonymous and hidden. A clearly defined ideology is much more vulnerable, because it is exposed to criticism.

C. IMPOTENCE

In its public structure, then, our modern technical and industrial society is a system with a hidden and anonymous ideology. The image of man and the social ideal with which it works are hidden and anonymous. In itself, this ideology would not be so bad, but it has for a long time been exerting a more and more powerful influence on the private sector of our society. As a consequence, attacks are always being made, from the private sector, on this ideology and the system that incorporates it. But the conclusion is inevitably the same—the unhappy discovery that the attack is bound to fail.

Again and again, revolutionary or non-conformist movements have arisen, some small, others on a large scale, engaging in battle against the inhuman ideological system of society, but they have all come to nothing. The first great attack was led by the socialist and Communist movements. In Western society, however, socialism has, after many difficulties and complications, become neatly integrated, via the trade unions and the political parties, into the social system.

A second assault on the ideology of Western society from the private sector took the form of a kind of ideological propaganda for the idea of the "community". This movement was given its initial impetus on the Continent by the spread of Ferdinand Tönnies' thought, as set out in his book *Gemeinschaft und Gesellschaft*. (The first edition of this work appeared in 1887 and it very soon achieved fame on the Continent.) Set against the inhuman "powers" of society as a whole (*die Gesellschaft*) were the healing and elevating forces of the small community (*die Gemeinschaft*). This was the period of the youth movement and the active social life of many different kinds of clubs and associations.

The powerful macrostructure of society was broken with the help of a great number of microstructures, which enabled man once more to be man, young people to enjoy the freedom of nature together and everyone who wished to escape from the matter-of-factness of modern life by mixing with friends and acquaintances with similar tastes and interests. There are even echoes of this romantic ideal of the community in the papal encyclical *Mater et Magistra*.[18] It is hardly surprising that the Church too was frequently regarded as a "community" of this kind at this time.

Unfortunately, quite apart from the fact that this community life is passing through a period of depression, it is true to say that the intimate community, association or club has had little or no real influence on the ideology and the system of the public sector of our society. It is, in fact, clear that these microstructures belong simply to the impotent private sector of society.

From time to time, pressure groups arise or charismatic leaders achieve prominence in society and, by active or passive resistance to the anonymous macrostructure, make a protest heard. They cause a stir for a little while, but life resumes its normal course very quickly. The real message of the protest is often nullified by the newspapers' treatment of such groups or individuals as sensational news. The *Nozem's* and *Provo's* in the Netherlands are making the intuitive protest of youth against society, but because these young people are not exactly sure what they are protesting against and what positive values they are really fighting for (what they say is often anarchistic or nihilistic) this revolt too is bound to end in nothing. The phenomenon of the beatniks in America passed into oblivion within a few years because it became fashionable, and the moment that something becomes fashionable, it is integrated into the pattern of society.

We are bound to recognize the fact that every attack

from the private sector on the problematic, inhuman and amoral ideology of the totally secularized macrostructure of our society has come to nothing. But we must go a little farther in our analysis. The Church does not belong exclusively to the private sector—as an institution, she is also embodied in the functional whole of our society. Perhaps without even knowing it, she has herself become a part of the anonymous system. It is possible to regard the private sector as an independent antipole to the objective and public system of society. In fact, however, the private sector has already been absorbed to a great extent in the system. The Church has a place within this system. I have already outlined the tasks assigned to the Church (and to religion in general). There is, however, one other task which the Church has been given in our society. There is one aspect of human life in the private sector which is feared in the public sector —fundamental uncertainty. I refer here to a special kind of uncertainty, since it is possible to insure against all the risks of life in our society. But there is one uncertainty which still remains and for which the public sector of society has no solution. That is the uncertainty which attacks the individual in his very existence—the uncertainty that is connected with the fear of death (and also irremediable misery and incurable diseases). If diseases and death were to be repressed by the ideology of the social macrostructure, a collective anxiety neurosis might well arise.

The Church is therefore the institution which accepts responsibility for caring for these deepest uncertainties of man, as the uncertain aspects of existence, death, suffering, disease and misery have been assigned to the Church and Christianity. But was it not Bonhoeffer who, during his imprisonment, was seriously concerned about a Church and a Christianity that functioned exclusively within the sphere of human suffering, weakness and uncertainty? (In this connection, Hoekendijk has referred to the Church's "sphere of pastoral scalping"!) He saw it as a danger to the relevance of God and Christianity in the modern world.[19]

The Church, therefore, appears to be the victim of a role

and a function which has been forced on her by society and which certainly minimizes her universal mission in the world. The question of the Church's future is a very serious one. If the Church continues to be and to do what she is now and what she has done up till now, then she has no future. Imperceptibly, she will come more and more to perform functional duties within a social order which is essentially tied to an unchristian ideology. In this way, she will gradually dig her own grave, which will at the same time be the grave of God. The situation is serious and what I have said should not be dismissed with an indulgent smile or a shrug of the shoulders.

We believe in the Church. We believe that she has a message to proclaim and a mission to fulfil with a future that is too great for us to imagine. On the other hand, however, we are confronted with a powerful social macrostructure with a hidden ideology which is at present leading mankind towards a doubtful future.

One-sided Pessimism?

I have, of course, laid myself open to the criticism that my view is altogether too gloomy. Surely our present-day social suprastructure is not in every respect debased, unchristian and immoral? It has, after all, provided us with very real welfare, abundant opportunities for improving our standard of living, humane and effective medical and social care and the technical means for a more pleasant way of life. Undoubtedly we lead a better, healthier and more fully human life than our ancestors in the pre-industrial age. And surely there is also a very strong humanizing tendency in our modern society?

None of these benefits can be disputed. It is possible to speak of our society as the field in which the roots of the wheat and those of the weeds are entwined with each other. As Christians, too, we are bound to admit that it is impossible to live in a state of absolute purity and without getting our hands dirty. At the last judgment, the tares will be separated from the wheat, but now we can only live in a morally

84

ambiguous situation, leading a twilight existence in which light and darkness are mixed.

This is a very common attitude towards our present situation and it would even seem to have a biblical foundation. But it should not be forgotten that the Bible also alludes to the fact that the grain of wheat can be choked and that the children of darkness are wiser than the children of light. A careful analysis of the situation has led me to conclude that the hidden ideology of the public sector of our society —and the public social structure itself—are at present threatening to choke Christianity, insofar as it has gained form in the churches. This ideology wears the sheep's clothing of "humanization" and thus threatens to blind us to its real form and content.

Secularization has liberated us from the mythical, metaphysical and religious explanations of the world. To judge from appearances, we are now free to choose which ideological interpretations of man and the world we wish to adhere to, because this is our own private affair. But this is in fact not the case—secularization imposes a new ideology upon us, but does this painlessly and imperceptibly. This ideology has a limited horizon which it tries to force upon us as the only horizon of human existence. It works with a hidden image of man and an idea of the "new world" which derive their power of attraction from the fact that they are so much a matter of course and at the same time so humane. It is an ideology which leads us towards a "better future", but which does not care to know whether man really has a destiny or not. Above all, it avoids making explicit questions about what man is and what his destiny is. Man's most profound questions must not be asked, because this would cause restlessness and uncertainty, both of which threaten the acceptance as a matter of course of the existing social system. The ideology of secular society therefore aims to deaden our deepest restlessness. In possession of society's means of communication, controlling the amusement industry and able to distribute "food and recreation", it can effectively direct our attention to questions of superficial and day-today interest only. The most profound question of all—the question about the very meaning of it all—must not be asked in the public sector. That would not be right! In the words of the sociologist A. Gehlen, there is in our modern world a "beneficent absence of questioning".[20] In this sense, Marx's phrase "the opium of the people" can be applied to the hidden ideology of modern society.

Another criticism that may be made of my assessment of the situation is that I am judging secularization, and especially secularization in the public structures of society, in the traditionally negative way and thereby betraying a secret desire to return to the old ideal of a "Christian society" of the kind that existed in the Middle Ages.

But it is impossible to return to this Christian past. The more optimistic analysts of the situation maintain that we have to accept the secular society of today and be alert both to the good that it has to offer and to the dangers inherent in it. We live in a new world and this means that yesterday's truth belongs irrevocably to the past. J. Sperna Weiland has said:

> The task of the Church, faith and theology in our present age is not to combat secularization and not to resist a development which has been going on for many centuries, a development which we are not undergoing, but in which we are taking an active part ourselves and which has led to the secular society because of a series of human decisions. If the gospel is still to be heard in this new world, then, from the human point of view, it will only be heard when we take as our starting-point the fact that we are living in a new situation in which the older truth no longer works and when we do not uphold yesterday's truth as the unchangeable message in the face of the truth of today and tomorrow.[21]

This rather abstract statement requires no further elaboration here. But it should be noted that it also contains the idea that all opposition to secularization in its contemporary form is the consequence of a rigidity in the proclamation of the Christian message and that this must be overcome. The

Church, faith and theology must go forward positively to meet the secular situation of today.

Secularization in Theological Discussion

The question of secularization has played a prominent part in theological discussion since the appearance of Friederich Gogarten's book, *Verhängnis und Hoffnung der Neuzeit. Die Säkularisierung als theologisches Problem* (Stuttgart, 1953). Gogarten insisted that a distinction should be made between "securalization" and "secularism". Secularization, in Gogarten's view, is the making worldly of the world, a process which was not only demanded by the Christian revelation, but was also first made possible by this revelation. Secularism, on the other hand, is a degeneration of secularization.

According to Gogarten, then, secularization is a necessary and legitimate consequence of the Christian faith. This faith has triumphed over the existing religious and mythical explanations of the world by conceiving the world as a *creation*. The Christian is therefore able to live in this world without mythical fear. In faith, the world is liberated in its worldliness and at the same time entrusted to man, who remains responsible to God alone in his cultivation of the world. The world is thus liberated in its worldliness while faith liberates itself from the world. Following a remarkably complicated line of argument, Gogarten concluded that true faith could only arise when the believer's attitude towards the world was secularized.[22] This secularized world, with its own worldly patterns of society and civilization, has therefore become the true place for faith.

Despite the fact that this attitude certainly gives the impression of being a theological justification of secularization made after the event, Gogarten's ideas did bring about a feeling of liberation in many theological circles. In a sense, he discovered the formula which enabled the Church to cease looking back regretfully to an ideal "Christian society" of the past and to see Christianity as a "service to the world", a world with its own autonomous progress through history to which the Church could adapt herself without fear and

The Grave of God

without a sense of frustration. The Church can therefore, in Gogarten's view, take her place among the many institutions of our pluralist society as a recognized partner.

Gogarten emphasized, however, that secularization was quite distinct from "secularism", which is a world order which leaves no room for faith, which does not tolerate the spiritual and religious freedoms of our pluralist society and which offers no positive support to the Church as one of the fundamental elements of that society. A society which is secularist in this sense gives free scope to ideologies which possess the power to assail the whole of human existence and to banish faith from society. Gogarten cites marxism, fascism and national socialism as forms of secularism which the Church and faith must constantly resist. There is, however, no objection to the Church's positive acceptance of secularization as such. Gogarten has therefore reconciled faith and the Church with the modern world.

The Catholic theologian Johannes B. Metz has to a great extent sided with the Lutheran Gogarten in a recent article, in which he said literally: "The worldliness of the world, which has come about in the modern process of secularization, has been brought about fundamentally (though not in its separate historical forms) not in spite of, but *by* Christianity. It is, in its origin, a *Christian* event."[23] The question, then, is why has the Church resisted this process of secularization for so long? Metz's reply is that this has happened because the Church has for too long clung to an outdated view of the world in Western history. In Metz's view, the Church has been engaged for so long in a hopeless battle with secularization because her thinking has until now been overshadowed by an almost purely medieval interpretation of the world. He does, of course, also put us on our guard against a false autonomy within this process of secularization.

These rather abstract theological reflections of Gogarten and Metz are of great importance and they have had a considerable influence on many Christian thinkers of today. Harvey Cox, for example, inclines to Gogarten's view in his book

88

The Secular City, although he has introduced several small distinctions. In the Netherlands, Dr A. Th. van Leeuwen has shown that he is, in this respect, a disciple of Gogarten.[24]

The positive values that are contained in the process of secularization—values that also apply to the Church and faith—have been obscured for too long. Only the disadvantages of the process were apparent whenever secularization led to painful consequences. The Church's loss of rights and possessions at the beginning of this century in France, for example, was lamented and condemned as a demoniac usurpation of power. Few Christians at the time realized that a weakening of the Church's position of power in the world at the same time released new spiritual and religious forces.

But, although the analyses which Gogarten, Metz and Cox have made of the situation are very valuable, they are in some respects unsatisfactory. In the first place, the proposition that secularization is demanded by the Christian revelation and is a consequence of the preaching of the biblical message has so far not been adequately vindicated theologically, though the view may well be substantiated in time by more convincing arguments. In the second place, however—and this is my main objection to these analyses—Gogarten and Cox do not seem to have perceived the growing power of secularism in a hidden and new form within the structures of our society and have consequently failed to provide a sufficient analysis of the true situation. They could combat marxism and national socialism openly because these were clearly recognizable ideologies. But they have not recognized the hidden ideology which pervades our modern society—the ideology which rots away the foundations of the Church and faith while these are outwardly treated with apparent respect in society.

The Struggle with the "Powers"

To summarize, then, we may say that the Church and Christianity originally submitted to secularization as a painful and pernicious dechristianization of the world, and have only recently begun to take up a more positive attitude towards this development. Secularization has furthermore led to a sharp division between man's private and public lives. It has resulted in a high degree of individual freedom in the private sector of society which can be used for man's creative self-development. There is, however, less freedom in life and work in the public sector of society since the whole of this sphere is dominated by objective structures, relationships and patterns of life and behaviour. The Church and faith have found a comfortable niche in the private sector which they now regard as their own particular sphere and missionary territory. This, however, is to some extent contradictory to the *universal* character of the Christian mission. The Christian is not called to bear witness only within his residential environment, within his clubs and associations and within his family. He is also called to proclaim the Christian message in his public life and in the macrostructure of society. But this has now been rendered impossible by the nature of this structure itself. It would seem that the Church has resigned herself to this situation. The true situation, however, is even more serious, since a hidden ideology which is totally unchristian *prevails* within the macrostructure of society and this ideology is creeping imperceptibly into the private sector of life, again in a hidden manner, and is thus beginning to prevail within the sphere which still remains open to the Church, although Christians are hardly conscious of these hidden powers as a latent danger.

What are we to do in this situation? The first thing is to be sober and watchful and to assess the situation as it really is. It is a remarkable fact that the New Testament and the early Church were deeply aware of the necessity to fight against invisible and hidden powers. Little or no attention has been devoted to these biblical data in the traditional theology and exegesis of the Catholic Church. Recently, however, the exegete Heinrich Schlier has written an excellent study on this subject.[25]

The teaching of the Bible about "principalities and powers" is, of course, combined with another element that is very difficult for us to accept today, namely that of the good and evil spirits. Clearly, there is a need for this New Testament world of spirits to be thoroughly demythologized. We are no longer required, in connection with our particular problem, to show that Satan is everywhere, in the manner of certain sects and fanatical religious leaders. We recognize that the New Testament authors tended to project good and evil in the world outside themselves and into a world of spirits because of the completely mythological climate in which they lived and their heritage of centuries of mythical thinking.

Nowadays, we are unable to accept this world of demons in the form in which it was to some extent taken for granted in the New Testament. We can, however, accept the essential content of this early Christian message, that is, that the Church and faith are constantly being put to the test by intangible and hidden "powers": "We are not contending against flesh and blood, but against the principalities, against the powers, against the world rulers of this present darkness, against the spiritual hosts of wickedness in the heavenly places . . ." (Eph. 6. 12), "the prince of the power of the air . . ." (Eph. 2. 2). According to Schlier, "heaven" and "air" here mean "the general spiritual climate which influences mankind, in which men live, which they breathe, which dominates their thoughts, aspirations, and deeds."[26]

The extent to which the hidden ideological power of our modern society to which I have already alluded coincides with the "powers" of the New Testament and primitive Christianity is clear from Schlier's description of the essence and the activity of these powers: "To influence nature so as to enhance their claims and authority over man . . . historical institutions and situations have thus become place and location, means and instruments of those powers." These powers can develop into "an ideology by means of which the authority of this [anti-Christian] state permeates everything, establishes itself and operates in all places." But: "When the principalities penetrate the world and the circumstances of human life in order to exercise their power through them, they thereby conceal themselves in the world and in the everyday life of mankind. They withdraw from sight into the men, elements, and institutions through which they make their power felt." Schlier's conclusion is expressed in a terse play on words: "To appear not to appear is part of their essence."[27]

I must, of course, emphasize that I do not regard the ideology that is prevalent within our society today as demoniac. I do, however, believe that we live far too little in accordance with the biblical and primitive Christian conviction of constant struggle against the hidden powers of our world and our society. The Bible warns us against these secret powers by calling them an adversary who "prowls around like a roaring lion, seeking some one to devour". But this warning is accompanied by the admonition "be sober, be watchful" (1 Pet. 5. 8). It seems to me that the Church has rather neglected this admonition. "Sober" in this context means that we should have no illusions about the "powers" and therefore take the reality of the situation fully into account without being in any way anxious. "Watchfulness" is a tireless alertness to the real course of events in the world.

Between a True and a False Future

As long as the Church—even after the reforms of the Second Vatican Council—continues to organize herself as a splendid and powerful institution and to emphasize her own prestige and influence in the world, as long as her fine and impressive façade is more important than what is behind that façade, as long as her own juridical structures count for more than the real human situation that she aims to set in order, as long as the Church regards herself as of greater consequence than the message that she has to proclaim and as long as her own renewal seems to her to be more urgent than the renewal of the world—as long as these attitudes prevail within the Church, then the Church will feel the need to be comfortably integrated, with the assurance of her own continued existence, within the structures of this world.[28]

But a Church that is unceasingly engaged in a struggle with the "powers" cannot lead a comfortable existence. A Church that is surrounded by the spirit of the "powers" has to live in the constant realization that she has received another Spirit. I hardly dare to say it, especially now, but Christianity can never allow itself to become entirely assimilated into a given historical situation. In other words, Christianity must always be to some extent a "stranger to the world". By this, I do not mean that the Church should cling to out-of-date structures and patterns of life and lament the process of secularization. No, Christianity is, in the ultimate and deepest sense of the phrase, a stranger to the world if it does not expect salvation to come from science and technology, a system of production, computers and planning.

It is, of course, true that Christianity and the Church must always be in history and that the Church must always be incarnate in this world. But at the same time it is also true that this incarnation can never be absolute. We are, in fact, in danger today of forgetting one aspect of Christianity, namely that the Christian message always points above and beyond any definite historical constellation. The Church can therefore never be completely assimilated into contemporary society because she *also* has the task of bringing this contemporary society under God's judgment. If the Church is forgetful of this task, in other words, if she relaxes her watchfulness and sobriety, then she will inevitably choose to become comfortably established within the constellation of the existing order. Consequently, her attitude will also become one of permanent compromise. This is one reason why the attics of the Vatican are full of the accumulated rubbish of centuries.

Whenever a choice has had to be made between the continued existence of the Church as a structure within a definite society and an attitude taken on principle towards the inhumanities of a régime, the choice has always been made in favour of the first. The French philosopher Merleau-Ponty believed that this formed part of the essence of the Christian Church when he referred to the impossibility of a Christian

93

rebellion: "There have been cases when the Church has supported rebels, because these have protected her temple, her ministers and her possessions. But God will fully enter history only when the Church is as conscious of her duty *towards all men* as she is of her duty towards her ministers, when she is as conscious of her concern for the houses of a threatened city as she is of her concern for her own buildings. There is therefore a Christian rebellion, but this is limited, and it occurs only when the Church herself is threatened."[29]

I believe, however, that this attitude does *not* form part of the essence of the Church. The Christian message is not meant to enter history only in a contemporary and adapted manner. It must always be in the nature of an "intrusion" into every historical situation. It is only if we see it in this light that we shall be able to understand that Christianity and the Church are not simply called upon to enter this period of history and this world with its social structures, but are also required to change them. In other words, the leaven must not disappear in the lump—it must transform it. Incarnation without transfiguration makes the Church and Christianity meaningless.

In its deepest essence, Christianity is the choice of a future for man and the world. This future is radically different from the future aimed at by the hidden ideology of our society. It is only Christian sobriety and watchfulness that can make us see that the life of the Church cannot be fully synchronized with that of the world. It is essential for us to see this, as it is a factor that is in constant danger of being forgotten whenever the problems of the Church and the world are discussed. We are, of course, bound to regret the isolation and the separation of a Church which has come to confront the world. It is, however, not so easy to know the alternative to this situation. Certainly this cannot be a Church which is fully assimilated into the world or which aims at complete integration. We are right to lament the fact that the Church and the world are divided, but this separation has come about because of the Church's rigid adherence to a past pattern of civilization. We must, however, be on our guard against accepting as our ideal the total integration of the Church and the complete bringing up to date of Christianity with the world. We must remain sensitive to those aspects of the Christian message that transcend every historical situation.

In the present secular situation, the Church is threatened by the hidden ideology of a social system. She has no future if she accepts the place accorded to her by modern society and if she—consciously or unconsciously—aspires to complete integration. If she is to have any part in the true future, she will have, in the deepest Christian sense of the word, to "empty herself". In the next chapter, I should like to discuss the real meaning of the Church's emptying of herself.

IV

The Church and Kenōsis

A. THE CHURCH

BEFORE explaining what is meant by the word *kenōsis* in the title of this chapter, I should like once again to consider the meaning of the word "church". The question of the Church's future amounts ultimately to this—how can the Church escape from the grasp, indeed from the imprisonment, of the hidden "powers" of a secular society? If her structure and form are firmly established like those of a house, then the Church will scarcely be able to escape a deadly fate. But do we necessarily have to think in terms of an original structure with a form that is subject to change? I propose to approach this problem along various paths.

The Use of Language in the Church

There are clear indications that both the appearance and the form of the Church are subject to change. This is apparent from the various ways in which the Church has understood herself in the course of history. This understanding has been expressed in a great variety of names for the Church and in the various ways in which the Church has been referred to.

"Church" is one of those strange words which is sometimes used in several different senses in a single sermon or discourse. When, for example, the phrase "our holy Mother the Church teaches . . ." is used, then the preacher is simply referring to the hierarchical sector of the community of the Church. On the other hand, a phrase like "the Church is today celebrating . . ." refers to the world Church and all her members.

These "manners of speaking" do, however, at the same time reveal something of the Church's understanding of her-

96

self. The first points to the existence of two groups of people within the Church—a teaching and a listening group, a group that is of age and a group that is under age, in other words, a hierarchy and a laity. Since the hierarchy can quite simply identify itself with the Church, this expression also contains the suggestion that the hierarchy is, so to speak, the Church of the front rank, whereas the non-hierarchical sector is only the second rank. I have accentuated this rather sharply so as to indicate the implications contained in such phrases as "our holy Mother the Church teaches . . .", but this does not mean, of course, that all these implications are always present.

"The Church is today celebrating . . ." appears to refer far more to the Church as the whole community of believers. Yet it does contain a remarkable element. It is, of course, familiar to most of us as a phrase used very frequently in the pulpit to announce a particular liturgical feast or to draw attention to the mood of a liturgical feast. But what is strange here is that the community of the Church has to be made conscious of the very celebration of something that it is in fact celebrating. Surely it would also be strange, or at least superfluous, if a speaker at a wedding were to say, "We are today celebrating a wedding". It is hardly necessary to stress, by an explicit announcement, what everyone present is obviously engaged in.

The real meaning, then, of the phrase "the Church is today celebrating . . ." is "the Church ought really to be celebrating today the feast of . . ., because this is what is indicated in the liturgical texts; these liturgical texts are, however, not directly accessible to you (the faithful) since they derive from an ancient tradition within the Church which is no longer alive but which must be brought to life again; I (the preacher) will therefore make it quite clear to you (the faithful) what we ought really to be celebrating today by virtue of an ancient tradition".

To take a single example, we need only to think of the catechetical difficulties involved when a preacher has to explain what the Church ought to be celebrating at Pentecost

97

to realize something of the tension that exists between "what ought really to be taking place" and "what is in fact taking place". A simple phrase like "the Church is today celebrating . . ." thus points to a contrast between the form of a Church community belonging to the remote past and the climate in which it lived and the Church community of today. In other words, it is quite obvious that there was at one time a different mode of existence within the Church which can only with difficulty, or cannot, be brought to life again, except perhaps in certain monastic communities, despite attempts to renew the liturgy and catechetical methods.

What's in a Name?

We can gain a better understanding of the great diversity of the Church's appearance throughout the course of history not only by analysing the use of language in the Church today but also by examining the various names for the Church.[1] The word "church" (*Kirche, kerk, kirk*) used in the Germanic languages is derived from the Greek *kuriakē*, meaning "what belongs to the Lord (*Kurios*)". Karl Barth and others have pointed to possible derivations from the Latin *circa* or *circulus*, referring to the semi-circular apse, where the faithful celebrated the Eucharist round the bishop.[2] The custom of calling the place where the Eucharist was celebrated the "church" may presumably also be derived from the same source.

The Romance languages use derivations (*église, iglesia, chiesa*) from another Greek word—*ekklēsia*. In Greek usage, *ekklēsia* had the meaning of an "assembly of people called together for the purpose of discussing state affairs". It was used in the Greek translation of the Old Testament for the Hebrew word *qāhal* which, with the customary addition of "Yahweh", also meant an "assembly of people called together", but in this case with the emphasis on the one who called the people together, namely Yahweh. In other words, the people of Israel, who were sighing in captivity in Egypt, were called together by Yahweh—through the medium of Moses—in order that they should make their way (the exodus) towards the promised land. In the New Testament, *ekklēsia* meant the people who were called together by Christ and who gathered in his name. It could be either the local church (even "where two or three are gathered in my name") or all the local churches together.

There are also very many other names in the New Testament which are used to indicate the Church more or less explicitly, for example, God's plantation, God's building, God's temple, the heavenly Jerusalem, the bride and the household and foundation of God.[3]

But the best known name for the Church is the "Body of Christ". This term originated with Paul and it occurs frequently in his letters. The precise sense in which Paul used this term is not immediately clear to us today because we think about a "body" in a totally different way. But Paul did, in any case, appear to wish to lay stress on two aspects of the being of the Church—firstly, the unity and the mutual solidarity of all believers in Christ (but not primarily in the sociological sense of a "corps") and, secondly, the glorified Christ's becoming already visible to faith. The Church Fathers elaborated this idea of the Church as a body as the image of mankind's becoming one. Man was inwardly torn and divided by sin, but the Church as the Body of Christ is "mankind's moving towards the unity of God . . . its transition from being torn and turned against the fellow man towards the new humanity, the union of those who are alienated from each other".[4] The Fathers also always saw the Church as a body in relation to the Body of Christ in the Eucharist. This is illustrated in William of St Thierry's statement: "Taking the body of Christ is the same as becoming the body of Christ."

What is remarkable is that, in the pre-scholastic period, the Church was called the "real body" of Christ and the eucharistic bread the "mystical body" (*corpus mysticum*). After the tenth-century controversy about Christ's real presence in the Eucharist, there was a change in the terminology. The Eucharist became known as the "real body" and the Church was called first the "Christian body" (*corpus christianum*) and later the "mystical body" (*corpus mysticum*).[5]

As a result of the conflict between the popes and the emperors in the Middle Ages, the word "body" came to be understood in a very juridical sense and to be used in determining the "rights of the Church". The external, juridical and institutional aspects of the Church were also emphasized in later periods (for example, at the time of the Reformation), with the consequence that, in 1966, it was possible for the Dutch bishops to write in their Lenten pastoral letter: "In the past, many Christians thought of the Church as an official, organized institution with a certain conviction of faith." The bishops then went on to point out that this idea of the Church was correct, but incomplete and they then referred to the view of the Church that was developed by the Fathers.

This very juridical and institutional view of the Church, which predominated for so long, was finally broken by the encyclical *Mystici Corporis* (1943), in which the "mystical" aspect of the Church was strongly emphasized. By "mystical", the encyclical meant that the Church was more than simply the total number of all the faithful—it was also a suprapersonal reality, one with Christ and inspired by the Holy Spirit and, as such, it could be said of her that she was "without spot or wrinkle and without blemish" (Eph. 5. 27).

Thus, a distinction was made between the Church's holiness and her sinfulness, between her state of being redeemed and her unredeemed state, between internal grace and external form, between what she is now and what she is to become and between what has already been fulfilled and what is still promised.

It would therefore be possible to write a history of the concept "body", of the way in which this word has been understood in the Church throughout time. The use of language in the Church—of a word or a name—does not mean that a reality has thereby been definitively determined. A name can, so to speak, lead its own life in history.

The People of God

I must now discuss a name that has only recently begun to live again in the mind of the Church—the "People of God".[6] This name for the Church is, of course, as old as the Bible itself,[7] but it has become rather overshadowed in the course of history. The conciliar theologian Yves Congar has spoken of a rediscovery of this idea of the Church as the People of God and has pointed out that it did not establish a really firm foothold in Catholic theology until the period beween 1937 and 1942. In the Vatican Council, the schema *De Ecclesia* did not originally include any chapter on the Church as the People of God. This section was inserted at the eleventh hour at the instigation of the co-ordinating commission.

The name "People of God" is obviously derived from the Old Testament. Applied to the Church, it stresses first and foremost the continuity between the Church and Israel. Israel's privileges can therefore be applied to the Church as well—her election, the Covenant and her dedication to God and to the promises. Another aspect that is emphasized in this name is the equality of all believers at the level of Christian existence. In accepting and fully appreciating the idea of the Church as the People of God, we are bound to reject the suggestion that the Church consists primarily of the hierarchy and secondarily of the laity and to stress the genuine and active participation of the whole "people", not only in the liturgy, but also in the entire life of the Church.

Above all, however, the name "People of God" points to a living, dynamic community of people, seeking and on the way towards what is already alive within the community in the form of a promise. The Church is not a rigid, fossilized and static institution, but a people on the way, on pilgrimage —a people that lives far more in tents than in temples. As the People of God, the Church is a historical event, a constant task,[8] and it is this aspect of the Church above all that makes a special appeal at the moment to all Christians who are concerned for the Church.

Theologians have, of course, been particularly engaged with the question of the priority of the names "Mystical Body" and "People of God". It cannot be denied that there is a certain tension between the realities indicated by these two names for the Church. Congar's tendency is to say that the People of God and the Mystical Body are complementary to each other. This implies a recognition of the existence of a one-sided view of the Church before the Council, despite a decided awareness of the tension between the Church as an institution (or corporeal reality) and as an "event".

I must also mention here another name for the Church which is apparently quite negative. Luther called the Church the "whore of Babylon". He was not particularly original in this—the poet Dante and the medieval theologian William of Auvergne had already "adorned" the Church with a title of this kind.[9] It is evident that this name refers to the Church in decline, the Church unfaithful to her mission. Such a term must be seen in the light of the Old Testament, in which Israel's infidelity to Yahweh was depicted in images of unchastity. Augustine, Origen and John Chrysostom saw Mary Magdalen as the image of the Church redeemed from sin, who was then designated as the "holy wench". Other writers (Bernard, Hildegard of Bingen) never referred to the Church in her period of decline as a "wench", but they did refer to her as a "desecrated bride". Bernard expressed this in an attractive play on words: "the bad shepherds 'prostitute' the Church instead of 'instituting' her".[10]

Finally, I should like to mention another faulty title for the Church—the "Kingdom of God". In the Eastern Orthodox Church, the Church is completely identified with the Kingdom of God and within the Roman Catholic Church there are many statements which tend to suggest this identification. This is, however, incorrect. The Church should be called the "opening phase of the Kingdom of God", the "becoming Kingdom of God" or even the organ and sign of the

Kingdom of God in this world.[11] The Kingdom of God is present in the Church, but always in the tension between what the Church is now and what she is to become.

In conclusion, we may say that the Church is, in her form and appearance, not a clear and defined reality. Even in her basic structure, the Church emerges in so many aspects and forms during the changing situations of history that there is no single moment of time at which her ideal form is realized. The name "Body" may at one point indicate the very deep unity of all Christians (and ultimately of the whole of humanity) in grace. In a period of conflict, the name may have a more juridical flavour and stress the rights of the Church. In the controversy with the Reformation, the external aspect of the Church tended to predominate, whereas, in a later period, the interior and mysterious inspiration of the body of the Church (*corpus mysticum*) is more emphasized. Again, the idea of the body of the Church can be interpreted in such a strongly institutional sense that it has to be corrected by the idea of the People of God on the way and the Church as an event and a task. Liturgical instruction tries to establish continuity between the way in which we think of the Church today and the traditional idea of the ancient Church ("the Church is today celebrating . . ."), but cannot cope with the fact that there is clearly discontinuity as well as continuity in the life of the Church. At one period of time, the Church could be identified with her hierarchical sector; in our own time, however, the equality of all members of the Church is predominant.

It is possible for the Church to appear differently in different historical situations because her fundamental pattern of life is sufficiently diverse to permit of such rich variety. Whenever she sees herself in a new way and has to develop a new form that will correspond to this new view of herself, she must always adapt, correct and reshape her structure. This will come, on the one hand, from the abundant possibilities contained within her fundamental pattern of life and, on the other, from the demands of the historical situation.

The Grave of God

The Choice of a Way

In all these changes in the Church's understanding of herself, it is possible to speak of different aspects of the Church coming to the fore. But it seems to me that, at a given moment in history, *a more fundamental choice* was made with regard to the form of life and the appearance of the Church. And precisely because this choice was made centuries ago it may still be hidden from us.

The way of history can be seen as a road along which we go forward and at the same time as a road which we make for ourselves. From time to time, we reach a parting of the ways. We then have to *choose* between two possible ways forward.

The Church came to such a parting of the ways in the fourth century. She was offered the chance of entering the political system of power embodied in the Roman Empire. Faced with the possibility of choosing between the prophetic servant-figure, the form of unpretentious service, and the political king-figure, the form of power and worldly distinction, she chose the second. This was the Constantinian turning-point in the Church's way. This choice may perhaps have been necessary at the time. It may even have been the right choice, since choosing the other road may have led to the Church's becoming an insignificant sect. But it certainly was a choice which determined the whole of the subsequent history of the Church. It resulted in the gradual emergence in the Church of thought and action in terms of power. By this I do not mean that the Church misused power, but that she tended to think from this time onward that the establishment of the Kingdom of God in fact meant the spread of the Church's power over the entire world. And at that time the "entire world" (*oikoumenē*) was the territory controlled by the Roman Empire. By securing a position of power for herself within that Empire, the Church had new and enormous opportunities for the establishment of the Kingdom of God on earth.

The idea of the Kingdom of God was, of course, understood

in the spiritual sense, but there seemed to be no objection to giving the spiritual mastery of the Kingdom of God an external and visible form as well. It is quite clear that a special interpretation of the "Kingdom of God" played an important part in the historic choice which centred in the Edict of Milan (313) at the time when this choice was made and subsequently. The many biblical texts referring to the royal power and dignity of Christ and his "Kingdom" were interpreted in a literal rather than in a metaphorical sense and conceived as referring to the worldly form of the Church and those who held office in the Church. It was not long before the Pope received the title of Christ from Apocalypse 19. 16—"King of kings and Lord of lords" (*Rex regum et dominus dominantium*). Two "kingdoms" continued, of course, to exist, but they could be dovetailed into one another; it was then quite clear that it was the Kingdom of *God* which had to be supreme in the form of the Church.

The Church gained enormous advantages from this choice. The most obvious was the very rapid spread of Christianity throughout the whole of the Roman Empire—in a very short time it was promoted from a cult that was simply "permitted" to the *cultus publicus*. Pagan tribes incorporated into the Empire by conquest were forced to accept baptism. Refusal often meant massacre. (I am not, of course, suggesting that this was one of the "advantages"!)

The disadvantages, which were as great as the so-called advantages, were revealed in the centuries that followed. The division of the Roman Empire into two parts in the tenth century led to schism in the Church. There were now two Christian Churches. The Western Church of the Roman patriarchate became organized, with the help of Charlemagne, within the Holy Roman Empire. The Eastern Church, on the other hand, became incorporated into the Byzantine Empire. Both claimed the title of the "one true Church of Christ". The Roman Catholic Church continued to maintain her position of power within the great Western Empire.

When the political power of the Empire declined at the

end of the Middle Ages, there was a corresponding deterioration in the Church's power. The one great Western Empire was torn apart by nationalism. Western Europe was divided into many different national states and European unity ceased to exist. In this sense, the Reformation was inevitable —a conclusion of political decline and of the Church's loss of political power. As long as the Church was a powerful presence in the Empire, schismatics and heretics like Jan Hus could still be burnt at the stake. In 1517, this was no longer possible.

Isolation

As I have already said in a previous chapter, the Catholic Church retired within her own walls after the Reformation. Political and geographical identification with a political system was no longer possible (although there are still visible remnants of the earlier constellation in some countries, such as Spain). But the old structures are still maintained within the Church. She is still divided and subdivided into territories of power (dioceses and parishes), although these frequently no longer correspond with the political territories.

The one missionary task of the Church is still subdivided into two. These are the two "powers" reserved for the clergy —the power of ordination (*potestas ordinis*), by which one is empowered and ordained to administer the sacraments and the "Word", and the power of jurisdiction (*potestas jurisdictionis*), by which one is empowered to exercise the pastoral *power* within a *definite territory*.

The emergence of the many national states created a danger for the emergence of national churches, a danger that was not illusory (Gallicanism, Febronianism and Americanism). The Church's authority and her jurisdictional power were therefore centralized in the Petrine office, and this naturally took place at the cost of the episcopal office. The First Vatican Council was thus a climax in this development.

While the Western world was developing—slowly and not without conflict—along democratic lines, the Roman Church continued to develop, perhaps even more emphatically, her feudal pattern of government, based on the idea of the supreme emperor with his dependent princes, with the inevitable consequence that she became more and more remote from the world. She took a defensive attitude towards the great social revolutions of the eighteenth and nineteenth centuries, continued to think and act in accordance with the feudal attitude towards power and, until as late as the last century, persisted in her attempts to restore the myth of European unity.

The reader may be tempted to comment at this point that the Reformation chose a new course. In one respect, this is true. But the Protestant Reformation is dialectically related to the Roman Catholic Church, and for this very reason it has always remained within the historical movement which began in the fourth century. It can therefore be regarded as a first attempt to create a more original kind of Christianity. This attempt was, however, frustrated because the historical movement of which the Reformation formed part did not reach its ultimate conclusion. The medieval attitudes towards power returned in different and milder forms (national churches, state religion and so on), even though many of the reformed churches are nowadays very democratic.

The modern historical tendency towards secularization is now almost complete. All attempts to interpret secularization positively as a "consequence of the preaching of the gospel" (Gogarten, Cox) are bound to strike us as rather questionable and they are certainly directly contradictory to the real course of events. The Church is no longer relevant in the great structures of modern society, but is imprisoned within the great system—a prisoner able to lead a harmless and comfortable enough life.

It may be a rather exaggerated comparison to make, but the Church is in a similar position to the Indians in the United States. Their way of life could not be made to fit into modern American society and they have consequently been put into special reservations where "they cannot do any harm". So it is with the Church. She has become a "religious reservation" with its own pattern of life. She can still exert some influence in the private sector of life, but outside this sector any effect that she may have is quickly neutralized.

We have at the present moment of history reached the point of bankruptcy, the legacy of the choice which the Church made at the parting of the ways in the fourth century. Then, the Church chose to follow a certain way in history. It is now obvious that this way is leading towards a dead end.

Return

What can the Church do then in such a situation? There is only one thing that can be done when you reach a dead end—return. But how can the Church turn round and go back along the path of history? (This, surely, sounds like Nicodemus' question!) She cannot, of course, do this literally. She must, however, look carefully back along the way she has come, as we have done very briefly here. She must discover the origin of the choice that has now led her to a position from which she cannot go forward. I have already suggested that this origin is to be found in a choice that was made in the fourth century. At that moment of history there was a parting of the ways—there was, in other words, another possibility. We must now try to establish what that other possibility was.

But, it will be asked, what sort of guarantee can we have that this other road does not also come to a dead end? We have no guarantee. All that we have are the promises of Christ and the task of being "on the way" as the People of God. We have no other possible choice but *metanoia*—to "turn round", to be converted, to choose the "other way".[12]

We can already see this other way indistinctly, and this is because the idea of the People of God was brought to life again and given prominence by the Council. If we regard the Church simply as a static, institutional "body", then a "return" is impossible. But understanding the Church as the People of God enables us to see her once again as a dynamic

108

reality, as a people that is moving and always on the way, a people that is constantly seeking, a people that can follow different roads and that can stray. Must we therefore say that the Church has followed the wrong way and, if she has, is this not in contradiction with the infallibility of the Church? I think not. What we are now experiencing is the Church's coming of age, her maturity. She *had* to follow this "wrong way" in order to come to a better and deeper understanding of herself and her mission. The Church has not wasted time or trouble in following the wrong ways that I have referred to. She has not simply wandered aimlessly around. She has had to follow this way (of suffering) in order to achieve greater spiritual maturity.

In the parable of the prodigal son, the father does not try to restrain his son when he wishes to set out on his journey. The son's road reaches a dead end, but he *returns*, inwardly mature and with even greater love for his father, to the "origin" of his way, to the original parting of the ways. He will now set out once more, but greatly enriched by all that he has experienced on the other way. He has not broken the link with his father. On the contrary, this link is greatly strengthened.

In the same way, the Church has not lost the inheritance of Christ on her "wrong way". She has not broken the link with grace. She too can set out again, enriched by her experience and purified by suffering. Her new way must be a genuinely Christian way. Does it exist for the Church? I believe that it does, and I have called it the way of *kenōsis*.

B. KENŌSIS

I have taken this Greek word from what was probably a hymn that was sung in the early Church. In any case, this hymn or canticle occurs in Paul's epistle to the Philippians. There, *kenōsis* means "emptying", and the passage in which it is found is: "(He) *emptied* himself, taking the form of a *servant*" (Phil. 2. 7).

It is easy to miss the deeper meaning of this text if the special value which is attached to the use of the word "servant" (or "slave") is not recognized. "Servant" became a very meaningful biblical concept thanks especially to the prophetic writings of the Old Testament, such as those of Isaiah. In four canticles, "Isaiah" saw the promised Messiah as the gentle and suffering "servant of Yahweh" (*'ebhedh Yahweh*).[13]

In the first part of the book of Isaiah, the Messiah is represented more as a king. These prophecies are presumably the work of Isaiah himself. The second part of the book (chapters 40-66) is sometimes called the "Second Isaiah" or "Deutero-Isaiah", and is probably the work of an unknown prophet since it relates to a much later historical situation, although tradition has attributed it to Isaiah.

These second prophecies provide us with quite a different picture of the coming Messiah. He is seen as the humble, gentle Servant of Yahweh, the chosen one who pleases Yahweh. He will not cry or lift up his voice and he will not break the bruised reed. But he will be a light to the nations, open the eyes that are blind and bring out the prisoners from the dungeon. Despised by men, he will, as the Servant of Yahweh, remain faithful to his mission. He will suffer, but he will not hide his face from shame and spitting. He will have no form or comeliness, no beauty to please us. He will be despised although he bears our griefs. He will be rejected, treated as one from whom men hide their faces (i.e. as a leper). Yet he will be like a lamb that is led to the slaughter. Broken by suffering and death, he will be an offering for sin and will lead many to justice. At the end, he will be raised and exalted by Yahweh.

It was this image of the Servant of Yahweh that the evangelists had in mind when they wrote the story of Jesus' life and it is also extremely probable that Jesus himself saw his life's task expressed in the image of the Servant of Yahweh.[14] At the beginning of Jesus' public life, an event took place, on the occasion of his baptism in the Jordan, that can be interpreted as a moment of revelation when Jesus became conscious of the nature of his mission. John the Evangelist here makes a clear reference to Isaiah's text of the Servant of Yahweh in making John the Baptist say: "Behold, the Lamb of God, who takes away the sin of the world!" (John 1. 29). Even more striking are Jesus' own words, which show how he identified himself more and more throughout his life with the suffering Servant of Isaiah.

Jesus saw his task as service: "The Son of man came not to be served but to serve, and to give his life as a ransom for many" (Mark 10. 45; cf. Isa. 53. 11). In Luke, this statement occurs at the Last Supper: "I am among you as one who serves" (22. 27). Although the Last Supper is represented in the synoptic gospels as a paschal meal, Jesus' words of consecration do not allude to the paschal lamb, but to the sacrifice of the Servant. The Matthaean and Lucan accounts of Jesus' temptation clearly reveal how Jesus chose the role of the gentle prophet who was exposed to contradiction in preference to a spectacular Messiahship.

Jesus did not, however, wish to confine the role of the Servant to himself—his disciples were also to be servants: "He who is greatest among you shall be your servant" (Matt. 23. 11). Paul described Christ's form of a servant and his self-emptying as a disposition which governed Jesus, and he called upon the Christians of Philippi to have this same disposition among themselves (Phil. 2. 5). The gesture of washing the disciples' feet—a task normally performed by slaves —was given a very special emphasis and interpretation by Jesus himself: "If I then, your Lord and Teacher, have washed your feet, you also ought to wash one another's feet. For I have given you an example, that you also should do as I have done to you. Truly, truly, I say to you, a servant is not greater than his master" (John 13. 12-17).

On the other hand, Jesus explicitly condemned all striving after honour, worldly esteem and power, everything, in other words, which was the opposite to that represented in the Servant (and I personally always find this text very disconcerting, as the word "scribe" can so easily be read as "clergy"): "Beware of the scribes, who like to go about in long robes, and love salutations in the market places and the best seats in the synagogues and the places of honour at feasts, who devour widows' houses and for a pretence make long prayers. They will receive the greater condemnation" (Luke 20. 46-47). In the words of Fr Schoonenberg, "The image of the Servant always points to the opposite of glory, to a self-emptying."[15]

We must now read Paul's *kenōsis* text in Phil. 2. 6-11 in the light of what I have said. I give the first four strophes of this hymn in a translation based on that of Fr Schoonenberg:

> He, who existed in divine form,
> did not pursue life as a prey
> at divine level,
>
> But *emptied* himself
> by taking the existence of a *servant* on himself
> and becoming equal to men.
>
> And, having appeared as man,
> he humbled himself
> by becoming obedient to death
> (to death on a cross).
>
> Therefore God has exalted him
> and given him the name
> which is above every name . . .

"Kenōsis" as an Existential Choice

Jesus' emptying of himself, as I have outlined it in the preceding section, has not been discussed in any great detail in Catholic theology. As Schoonenberg has pointed out, the whole text has been interpreted far too much in the light of the doctrine of the two natures, as defined at the Council of Chalcedon. The point of departure has consequently always been that the opening words of this hymn refer to Christ in his existence as the Word of God, that is, before his incarnation. It was, then, the Word of God who emptied himself of the glory inherent in the divine nature and who took on the form of a servant by becoming man. According to this interpretation, then, Christ's self-emptying refers to a choice made in the divine sphere, before the incarnation.

This interpretation need not be entirely excluded, of course, but it is far more probable that Jesus chose to empty himself during his life on this earth. This view is reinforced if a comparison is made between the various kenotic texts found in the New Testament. It is clear from these that Jesus always chose the form of self-emptying, the form of the Servant, whenever he was placed in any situation demanding such a choice. In the desert, for example, he rejected the way offered to him by Satan ("The devil . . . showed him all the kingdoms of the world . . . and said to him, 'To you I will give all this authority and their glory . . .'" Luke 4. 5-6). He defended his acceptance of suffering when questioned by Peter. He said that he had come not to be served, but to serve. He chose the cross rather than the joy that was his due. He did not choose his own will, but the chalice that the Father gave him to drink.

All the texts can therefore be interpreted in the light of decisions made *within Jesus' human existence*.[16] There are thus clear indications that the *kenōsis* text of Philippians 2 should also be interpreted in this way.

The question now is, of what did Jesus empty himself during his life on this earth? His divine origin and the mission that he had received from God to establish the Kingdom of God meant that he could have presented himself to the world with a great display of dignity and royal power and majesty, in other words, "life at divine level" (Phil. 2. 6). This was a very real possibility for him. His brothers, after all, urged him to seek publicity and go to Judea, "that your disciples may see the works you are doing. For no man works in secret if he seeks to be known openly. . . . Show yourself to the world" (John 7. 3-5). The Zealots, a party composed of Jews who were opposed to Roman rule, enjoyed a great deal of support among the people. After the miracle of the feeding of the five thousand, they tried to make him the Messiah, a role that would at the same time have incorporated an act of resistance against the Roman rulers. Jesus, however, avoided this possibility, as if it were a temptation. It is worth remembering, however, that the role of royal Messiah must have appealed to Jesus as a real opportunity to establish the Kingdom of God. His avoidance of this possibility does not therefore mean that he regarded this role as sinful.

> Our best approach to the secret of Jesus is to say that he refused the function of a political messiah because he felt himself called by the Father to be a prophet. For him it was a higher vocation to be the Servant of Yahweh than to be the son of David. . . . When Israel in exile cherished the image of the Ebed Yahweh, the Servant of Yahweh, as the ideal, it had reached a greater maturity through the Spirit than when it gave rise to the image of the theocratic Messiah. . . . God finds a more direct approach to the human heart through the meekness of the prophet than through the power of the king, even when this king does justice to the poor. It is precisely this supremely human way of the defenceless word, embodied in a whole person, which is stronger than any political power. . . . Together with this rejection of power, Christ obviously rejected by the same token all lust for power and all abuse of power.[17]

For Jesus, then, *kenōsis* meant an emptying of himself of every urge for power and self-importance and of all concentration on himself. As the Servant of Yahweh, he aimed to become completely absorbed in being the mediator between the Father and his brothers, an attitude which comprised the whole of his life and, if necessary, included the death on the cross.

The way of *kenōsis* meant for Jesus a definite choice within his life on earth. Two ways were open to him—he was at the parting of the ways in his life. Rejecting political leadership, he chose the role of the defenceless prophet. He gradually came to recognize that this choice demanded one thing of him—that he should follow the way of the Servant of Yahweh to the farthest limit, the martyr's death, in order to "make many to be accounted righteous, and he shall bear their iniquities" (Isa. 53. 11). The paradox is that Jesus, who did not pursue life at the divine level, but chose the way of the gentle, suffering Servant who sacrificed himself for others, did not obscure his divine form in so doing. In emptying himself, he revealed in the most profound way his divinity and the divinity of the one who had sent him.[18] "For God is love . . . In this is love, not that we loved God but that he loved us and sent his Son to be the expiation for our sins" (1 John 4. 8-10).

"Kenōsis" as the Church's Way

I have dealt at such length with the biblical theme of "self-emptying" so that we should be able to sense the deeper meaning of this mystery of Christ, since everything that I have said about it must also be applied to the Church. The life of the Body is the same as that of the Head—the Bride follows the Bridegroom. If the Church is to have a future, she must renounce all claims to power and all longing for power, all honour, worldly esteem and love of display. For Christ's sake, she will have to become "poor" in the deepest evangelical sense of the word. In order to win everything, she will have to be ready to lose everything. She will have to be a *Servant*—a Servant who will not use power to force men to action, but who will aim to rule only by love.

Do not imagine that this call to the Church to accept the kenotic form of Christ is exaggerated. The crisis in which the Church finds herself at present is very serious indeed. The Church's "way" of the royal figure of power has now almost come to a dead end. If she attempts to continue along this way, then there is a very real danger of going astray. The danger of a break in the links with her "origin" is very great today. We—the Church—are being drawn along in a mighty and overwhelming process, a secular dynamism which looks to the future and never looks back. The social system and its hidden ideology is threatening to swallow the Church up.

Most of those who are alert to the danger seem afraid to make any radical change and simply advocate "adaptation" or spectacular novelties. We must, they say, adapt ourselves to the inevitable situation and then make the best of it.

Paul van Buren (see Chapter I) accepts the empirical thinking that prevails in our modern industrialized society as a necessary point of departure and then goes on, with grandiose professional skill, to attempt to apply the method of linguistic analysis to the gospel. With a certain pride, he shows that something of the gospel still remains at the end of this process.

Bultmann accepts the Church's exile in the private sphere of life and concentrates on "faith" as the existential attitude of the individual in a splendid and Christian analysis of the situation. But his thoughts about the Church are vague and inadequate.[19]

Tillich takes as his starting-point the questions that are implicit in our present situation, but the problematical aspect of the situation itself and of the limitation of the questions asked is not discussed.

An ecumenical theologian such as the Czech Hajdanek summarized this attitude very well in a recent article. He maintains that the Christian message must be reinterpreted so that it becomes "a reflection at the level of modern thinking, a non-religious, social and secular reflection which has some meaning for modern man and which appeals to him and convinces him".[20] Although these words are well meant, I detect in them the suggestion that we must *at any price* go in for spreading the Christian message, no matter how, so long as we somehow appeal to modern man.

The Catholic Church was also alert to the danger and a Council was summoned. The real aim of the Council only became clear to the Fathers during the course of the sessions. The Council has been seen above all as a renewal of the Church, and no one will deny that a great deal has been achieved. The word *aggiornamento*, first used by Pope John, became the symbol of the whole movement of renewal within the Church. The literal meaning of *aggiornamento*, however, is "adaptation to the modern age" and, for this reason, the word was a very unfortunate choice. The word that should really have been used was not *aggiornamento*, adaptation or renewal, but *kenōsis*.

The only Christian who has so far expressed a more radical attitude towards the way of the Church is Bishop John Robinson, in his book *The New Reformation?* In this book, he maintains that there must be a "stripping down" of the Church—the Church must strip herself of everything that bestows privilege and prestige on her with regard to the world. This is undeniably the kenotic principle. But Robinson believes that we can work on two sides simultaneously and that we can learn to live in an overlapping situation.

It is certainly true to say the Reformation discovered the kenotic principle for the Church. Among other things, the Reformation was a revolt against the power of the Church. That is why the preaching of the reformers stressed a *return* to the purity and simplicity of the gospel. Their revolt, however, was one-sided and led to an ambivalent concept of the Church—the real Church remained invisible. We may indeed wonder whether this one-sidedness did not eventually lead to a return of rigid institutionalization, in a different and more hidden form, in the reformed churches of today.

We may conclude by saying that the critical situation of the Church has, generally speaking, been widely recognized, but that its deepest causes have not been sufficiently understood. The "solutions" that have so far been suggested are inadequate. The Church is still threatened. The way of *kenōsis* has been discovered, but we have not yet set out on it.

Why has the Church not chosen this Way before?

We must now attempt to answer the question, why has the Church not returned from her wrong way and why has she not chosen the way of self-emptying before? To solve this problem, the New People of God must consult the Ancient People of God. It was only through the purification brought about by suffering in exile that Israel came to understand the true nature of her election and the real form of the Messiah.

After their deliverance from captivity in Egypt and the conquest of the Promised Land, the Ancient People of God looked forward to a comfortable and settled existence in the new country. They wanted to make sure of a long history ahead of them. They also wanted to be respected by their neighbours, to have a king like the other nations surrounding them. There were, of course, objections to this—was not Yahweh the only king of Israel? (1 Sam. 8. 7; 12. 12). Yahweh, however, did not prevent them from going the way they wished to go and gave them a king.[21]

This monarchy reached its climax in the splendour and magnificence, the power and the esteem of the royal court of Solomon. It was followed by division, the mental and geographical rift which terminated in the Babylonian captivity. Israel became the victim of power politics and was in danger of being swallowed up as a nation by a strange people. Israel's national and religious consciousness was kept alive only by the prophets. At first, the people placed their hope in the coming of a Messiah who would free them, and thought of this Messiah as a king, a theocratic figure, a military leader. But suffering purified and matured Israel and the image of the Messiah in the form of a Servant gradually clarified in the mind of the people. This is the *'ebhedh Yahweh* described by the anonymous prophet, the Second Isaiah, in the four canticles of the Old Testament.

The New People of God, the Church, *had* therefore first of all to follow the way of power, magnificence, esteem and majesty. Now, however, she has also been purified in the "exile" of a world in which God has for a long time been dead and in which she and her form of power have become irrelevant and out of date, a world which either does not hear her preaching or does not understand it. In present-day society, she is threatened by ideological and structural "powers". This, then, is the time of the Church's purification, the time in which she can at last become aware of the way of *kenōsis*.

This way of self-emptying is also far closer to the authentic way of Christ than that of royal power, because it is the way of the cross and of the resurrection. Self-emptying and humiliation were the fate of the Servant of Yahweh.

Christians sometimes become seriously disturbed because the Church is no longer respected, because she is despised or simply ignored. But these form an essential part of the way of *kenōsis* and the cross. They are essential aspects of the fate of the Servant of Yahweh, who had no form or comeliness and no beauty, and was despised and rejected by men (Isa. 53, 2-3). Christians behind the Iron Curtain therefore lost heart at first when the Church in the Soviet satellite states lost all her external claims to power, all outward form and beauty after 1945. Whenever the Church automatically identifies herself with her firmly established and highly respected external form in society, then it is quite possible for it to appear as though the loss of this form is the end of the Church herself. This happens when the Church's way of *kenōsis* and the cross has sunk into oblivion, since it is precisely in emptying herself that the Church can reveal her real glory.

The hymn of *kenōsis* in Phil. 2. 6-11 includes an "imperative", the suggestion of a mysterious law, in the statement which follows the words about self-emptying—"Therefore God has exalted him" (2. 9). *Now* the Servant of Yahweh is despised and rejected, but "Behold, my servant shall prosper, he shall be exalted and lifted up" (Isa. 52. 13). Thus, the Church may also know that she will become worthy of the promises of Christ by following the way of *kenōsis*. The essence of being a Christian is having faith in the future through resurrection.

"Kenōsis" in the Tradition of the Church

Finally, we may wonder whether the way of *kenōsis* has not always remained alive in the mind of the Church. Yves Congar somehow suggests this in his book, *Power and Poverty in the Church*.[22] He shows himself to be a good apologist for the Church when he tries to prove that "through the centuries the hierarchy of the Church has shaped her life by the ideal of service she received, as her law, from the Lord and the apostles". But he does not provide this proof. On the contrary, his argument seems to prove the very opposite.

The testimonies provided by the first four centuries of Christianity of the Church as a servant are most impressive, but speaking about the medieval Church, Congar says that "the word *ecclesia* indicates not so much the body of the faithful as the system, the apparatus, the impersonal depository of the system of rights whose representatives are the clergy or, as it is now called, the hierarchy, and ultimately the pope and the Roman Curia". And he continues:

> I would like to point out in this respect a problem which, as far as I know, has never been considered, namely the application of the directives of the Gospel, not only to individuals but to the Church as such. Is it the individual alone who must be the servant and not the master, who must forgive offences, bless his enemies and not curse them? Have themes such as these any longer a place in an ecclesiology identified in practice with a treatise on public ecclesiastical law?

The Church has, however, followed a different way since the first four centuries of Christianity and this has resulted in the growth of a different tradition. In the medieval Church, "the authority of God [was] seen as wholly, one might almost say physically and automatically present, in the authority of the Church; the absolute standard of the divine authority [was], so it would seem, identified with and invested in the human standard of the ecclesiastical authorities." Congar goes on to emphasize this discontinuity with the past by saying: "It is obvious that this development would scarcely have been possible if there had been no progress beyond the ancient meaning of *ecclesia* as indicating the Christian community." Congar therefore concludes that a new way must have been followed since, in our own time, the Church is "called upon to make a clean break with the old forms of her presence, heirlooms in the world, legacies from the days when she controlled the hand that bore the sceptre, and to find a new style of being present to men."[23]

No, there is no continuous tradition of the ideal of *kenōsis* and service throughout the centuries in the structures of the Church. But this does not mean that there has been no awareness of this ideal within the Church. Charismatic and prophetic figures have kept the lamp of this kenotic tradition burning, although sometimes it was no more than a tiny flame. What is more, the choice of the way of power has always been dated back to the Constantinian turning-point in the fourth century.

The great medieval mystic, Bernard of Clairvaux, wrote, for example, to Pope Eugenius III (who had been a brother of Bernard's in the Cistercian order): "You let yourself be overwhelmed by judgments that you must pass in all kinds of external and worldly matters. I hear of nothing but judgments and 'laws' from you. All that, and striving after esteem and wealth, comes from Constantine, not from Peter."[24] This idea is expressed even more concretely in the following statement taken from another letter which Bernard wrote to Eugenius: "If the Pope dresses in silk, covers himself with gold and precious stones, surrounds himself with soldiers and servants and rides on a white horse, he more resembles the successor of Constantine than the successor of Saint Peter."[25]

Revival

The lamp of the kenotic tradition, then, was not completely extinguished and was therefore able to blaze up again at the Second Vatican Council. There, the world witnessed the remarkable phenomenon of the Pope and various bishops apparently becoming once again aware of the kenotic form of the Church. The theme of the Church's "self-emptying" (often expressed as the "Church of the poor") and of her being a servant was stressed with unwonted and often extreme force.

On 20 October 1962, the Council turned to the world with the following message: "Far from turning away from our worldly tasks, our attachment to Christ in faith, hope and love places us entirely *at the service* of our brothers, in accordance with the example of our Master, who 'came not to be served but to serve'. The Church was therefore made not to rule, but to serve."

In his Christmas message, Pope John spoke about "the Church which was not made to rule, but to serve the nations". Cardinal Frings of Cologne said in his Lenten pastoral letter of 1963: "Holding office in the Church does not mean ruling, but serving the well-being of the faithful."

It is interesting to observe how the bishops stressed the theme of service in the pastoral letters that they addressed to their dioceses after the first sessions of the Council. Mgr Guerry, the archbishop of Cambrai, wrote, for example: "A first principle of the gospels is that authority should not be regarded as ruling, but as service. How often (!) the Council Fathers have quoted in their interventions the words of the Redeemer, 'I came not to be served but to serve'." Cardinal Archbishop Gerlier of Lyons touched on the theme of self-emptying when he wrote to his diocese: "As a bishop, I cannot simplify everything in a day, but I continue to question myself about the clothing which custom obliges me to wear at liturgical ceremonies and elsewhere, about the honours which are bestowed on me during services and in everyday life. . . ."And Mgr Mercier, the bishop of Laghouat, wondered whether "the corps of bishops should not take the initiative towards a voluntary detachment from everything that still remains of outward signs of wealth and a temporal power that has now fortunately passed away?"

The whole corps of bishops did not go so far as to do this, but certain individual bishops did in fact reply to this question. In the Lenten pastoral letter of Cardinal Frings from which I have already quoted, there was an explicit reference to the "choice" of the fourth century: "The various outward signs and ceremonies which exalt the person of the bishop have appeared in the house of history, especially at the time of the Emperor Constantine, when the marks of honour to which the high officials of the Roman Empire were entitled were defined and when these honours were extended to the bishops. The Church can, however, be understood without these outward distinctions of honour. Wherever there is persecution, she has to do without them, and this does not harm her inner life." Perhaps the sharpest

and most concrete pronouncement against the Church's form
of power and prestige was spoken by Mgr Juan Iriarte, the
bishop of Reconquista in Argentina: "We have to proclaim
the Christian Message from the height of our marble altars
and episcopal palaces, in the incomprehensible baroque of
our pontifical Masses and in the even stranger definitions of
our ecclesiastical language, while we appear before our
people clad in purple . . . and our people, when they meet us,
call us 'Your Grace' and genuflect to kiss our ring! It is no
easy task to free ourselves of this great weight of history
and custom."[26]

Finally, in an interview with Michel van der Plas, the late
bishop of 's Hertogenbosch, Mgr W. Bekkers, referred to the
kenōsis text of Phil. 2 and commented on it thus: "In
Christ's complete emptying of himself—and by this I mean
not only his death, but also his, so to speak, keeping low
company with man—we must look for the poverty of spirit.
And we have to imitate this at our own level *by an analogous emptying of ourselves*."[27]

"Kenōsis" is Exodus

There is a polarity between the content of these texts and
the reality of the Church here and now, between the hearing
of the word and the doing. How are we to become, not
simply hearers that forget, but doers that act? (James 1.
22-26).

How is the Church to change herself and her direction
and follow the way of *kenōsis*? How is she to empty herself
of her form of power? How is she to escape from the grasp
of the structures of society and their hidden ideology? These
are the questions that immediately spring to mind, and we
have to admit that we cannot provide any ready answers
to these questions as to *how* the Church is to achieve all
this. We have at the moment no charismatic leader to show
us what we have to do. Is the Church then, despite the
adjustments that have been made by the Council, to pursue
her course to the bitter—and absurd—end? Must she, like
the grain of wheat falling into the ground, first die before

she bears fruit? Or is it possible to make her conscious of the new way of *kenōsis* in such a way that she will risk undertaking the Exodus, choose this new direction and follow it?

The whole of my study of this problem contains the hidden hope that this is possible. In the next chapter, then, I shall try, tentatively and exploratively, to discover what *kenōsis* ought in fact to mean for the Church.

V

The Future of the Church

So far we have established that the question about the
Church's future could be asked because the Christian faith
and the Church's confession of this faith are in a critical
situation. At first sight, this situation appeared to be connected with a crisis concerning the idea of God and the way
in which the Christian message was being proclaimed. Closer
examination of the problem, however, revealed that it is
connected with the appearance of the Church herself.

Secularization and rapidary development in our world are
the causes of the Church's increasing irrelevance in our
modern urban, highly populated, cybernetic, socially and
economically interdependent and mobile society. The Church
has been driven into the purely private sector of this society,
where she seemed at least to be assured of an independent
existence. But even this is threatened by the hidden ideological "powers" of the macrostructure of society.

The various theological attempts to solve the problem of
secularization have all been inadequate. The movement of
Christianity in history cannot be synchronized with that of
the secular dynamism of the future. The only possible way
for the Church to escape from the world's "powers" is the
way of kenōsis—she must empty herself of all claims to
worldly power. She must accept the form of the prophetic
Servant of Yahweh without fearing the world's scorn.

I now propose to put forward the outline of a concrete
plan of the Church in her kenotic form. I must, however,
emphasize that I am making no claims whatever with this
plan. It is offered merely as suggested material for discussion.
A draft plan of this kind is always open to changes and
modifications. Although I have not written everything that
follows in the form of questions, it should be seen as one

125

great, but serious question put to the whole community of the Roman Catholic Church.

Self-emptying of Forms of Power

First and foremost, the "visible nature of the Church" must be expressed in a new way. It is impossible to find any justification for making the Church visible in the form of royal power, let alone for the Pope and the bishops appearing in the splendour of Renaissance princes. The Church is primarily visible in the community of people which she constitutes on the basis of word and sacrament. This community of course includes those who hold office in the Church, those men who have been called and empowered to administer the word and the sacraments of the Church and to achieve single-mindedness among her members.

I am therefore convinced that all princely splendour and magnificence is contrary to the kenotic form of the Church and may as well disappear. If we are really to take the way of *kenōsis* seriously, a number of radical "emptyings" will have to take place.

In the first place, it seems to me that the Pope should give up the "ecclesiastical State". It is in itself remarkable that the bishop of Rome—in the formal sense—does not reside in Rome, but in another State. All so-called speculations about the Church's possession of her own State property as an essential condition for her existence must be regarded as tendentious. There can, of course, be no objection to the Church's retaining the Vatican as private property. But the organization of this little piece of ground as a miniature State with its own "government", parliament, army, system of taxation and State officials is contrary to the Church's form of *kenōsis*.

Once the ecclesiastical State has been allowed to disappear, there should be no need to send any more diplomatic representatives from the Vatican to the various governments. The papal nunciatures could be discontinued and the Vatican School of Diplomats could be closed. In passing, it should be noted that this would free a number of priest-officials, who could then be used to supply the shortage of priests engaged in pastoral work in the diocese of Rome.

I should also like to suggest that the Pope should leave the Vatican Palace and find a more simple dwelling in the city of Rome. At the same time, he could also use a simpler church of St Peter as his episcopal church. The "old" church of St Peter could perhaps best be set up as a museum, a monument to the time when the Church had a different form. This must, of course, seem pretty radical, but it would not change anything that is essential to the Church and would, on the contrary, reveal more clearly than ever before the true form of the Church.

The primacy of the Pope should be stripped of all the forms which make it seem analogous to the primacy of the emperors in relation to their princes. The true nature of the Petrine office can only be revealed if it is emptied of all its imperial distinguishing marks. The papal tiara with its triple crown could then be set aside, since the Pope would have renounced one of these crowns. It is, of course, not simply a question of the tiara—the whole question of ecclesiastical dress must be gone into with the aim of making it simpler and less extravagant and of doing away with all items that are suggestive of the royal or imperial court. I do not intend to make any concrete suggestions about how the new dress should look—there are very many possibilities here.

This emptying of the Vatican's display of power and of the outward form of the papacy must, of course, be accompanied by a similar emptying of the outward form of the episcopacy. It is quite clear from the many quotations at the end of the previous chapter that many of the bishops are already well aware of the need for *kenōsis* in this sphere. The real nature of the bishops' office will also be expressed far more clearly once this office has been "emptied". What is more, ecumenical dialogue about "ministry in the Church" will be able to move on to a higher plane as soon as the papal and episcopal offices have been stripped of their princely forms of power (dress, signs of honour, behaviour, palaces and so on). In this connection, I am reminded of what a well-known commentator on ministry in the Church, Dom Gregory Dix, has said—that ecclesiastical office is the ecumenical problem number one.

This also implies that the two "powers" that are inherent to the ecclesiastical office (the powers of ordination and of jurisdiction) must be given a different emphasis. Should we still continue to speak about "powers" (*potestates*)? In the "imperial form" of the Church, it is obvious that these two aspects of the Church's ministry should be translated into terms of power, but I do not believe that this is in itself necessary. Ministry in the Church is essentially a service (*ministerium*) to the believing community.

This does not mean that no authority is entailed in the Church's ministry. The real problem of authority is that it has, in the past, been understood in too mechanical and juridical a sense, as though sacramental consecration automatically and by virtue of "law" constituted the authority of the office-bearer, who could consequently exercise power or refuse to exercise it, quite arbitrarily and according to his own personal view, over the faithful (both with regard to external actions and with regard to the conscience), who were expected to obey him blindly. The authority of God and of Christ were, so to speak, seen as the personal possession of the office bearer, and the Christian, in obeying the office-bearer, was obeying God and Christ. Such a mechanical (and indeed, almost physical) conception of the authority of the Church's ministry is no longer tenable. It is quite obvious from history that this view has, among other things, led to the abuse of authority. The corresponding idea of obedience as an absolute subjection of the will (which is often also extended to a subjection of the intellect) is not derived from the gospels, but from the relationship between a prince with absolute authority and his obedient "subjects".

Authority in the Church's ministry stems from sacramental ordination, in which the office-bearer receives special help, by the laying on of hands and prayer to the Holy Spirit, to carry out his ministry. He is then chosen by the believing community (the Church) to make the saving work of Christ actual for that community. He is therefore given the task of preaching the Word and of administering the sacraments. He is, however, not free in this task, but is bound, like all other believers, in obedience to the gospel. He is placed in office by the spiritual gifts (charismata) of the office and by the choice and commission of the believing community of the Church. He is therefore not simply one who carries out what is alive in this community. He can only fulfil his ministry if he also listens to what is alive in his flock (to what the Holy Spirit is saying in his believing community, the Church) and verifies what he hears, by virtue of the authority vested in his office, against the gospel. He must, in other words, "distinguish the spirits" and only then give guidance and take decisions with authority in the name of the believing community.

This is the difficult and laborious service which the office-bearer has to carry out in the believing community. We ought therefore to speak, not of the "power of ordination", but rather of the office, the service or the ministry of ordination (*ministerium ordinis*).

The other aspect of office in the Church is the preservation of unity in faith and of single-mindedness or unanimity within the community. This too is above all a service to the community. It *cannot* be accomplished by the sort of power exercised by a judge or a ruler. History has shown that decrees and police activity have never achieved unity and unanimity. Examples of this are numerous—the Inquisition, imprisonment, torture, burning at the stake, trial and conviction without defence, unmotivated excommunication and suspension, and so on. However, the service to the unity of the flock was described by Jesus himself in the parable of the lost sheep and the good shepherd. We should note that the good shepherd of this parable does not use force to drive the sheep back to the flock—employing, so to speak, a strict power of jurisdiction—but rather shows his service to the flock by going after the lost sheep with loving concern and "when he has found it, he lays it on his shoulders, rejoicing" (Luke 15. 5).

This aspect of office in the Church should therefore be known as the pastoral office, service or ministry (*ministerium pastoralis*).

Territorial or Personal

This automatically leads us on to the question as to how this pastoral office ought to be carried out in a kenotic Church.

It is well known that, when the present canon law, which dates from 1918, was being drawn up, there was a strong movement in favour of associating the laws of the Church not with territories, but with persons. One of the advocates of the "right of the person" was the young canonist Mgr Pacelli, who later became Pope Pius XII. The case was, however, won by those who supported the territorial right with its long tradition and henceforward the idea *leges sunt territoriales* was in force. I shall not go into the views that prevailed at that time in connection with the personal right here, but should simply like to put forward, as a suggestion, that the territorial organization of the Church's dioceses and parishes should now be abolished. This territorial system, which is so reminiscent of the ancient feudal structure of the Church, can often be defended only on a basis of historical arguments. It seems absurd that a thinly populated territory can have its own diocese simply because it was at one time a principality.

We must take as our starting-point the idea that was formulated at the Council—that the Church is the sacrament of salvation for the world. The Church must therefore be a *sign* of redemption *for the world*. This means that we take into account the structure of the modern world, which consists above all of large urban agglomerations. The Church has therefore to direct her attention in the first place to the great metropolises, conurbations and other forms of town and city life. The Church must consider these great towns and cities, insofar as they form a single political, social and economic entity, as one single pastoral task with many pluriform subdivisions. It is not enough to try to approach the modern city-dweller via the parochially organized residential suburbs.

This would restore to the word "bishop" the literal meaning of the original Greek *episkopos*. This word means "overseer" (F. van der Meer has translated it as "looker upon"). Its Latin equivalent is "superintendent". Thus, the Church ought not to confine her activity to arbitrarily divided residential districts on the periphery of the town, but first have a complete oversight of the town's structure—its industries, the functioning of its business life, its educational institutions, the forms of its cultural life and its services, its social stratifications, the place and the special problems of its youth, workers, officials, technologists, intellectuals and old people and so on. The bishop-overseer, with his brothers in office (the priest), must therefore have a complete view from above of the multiplicity of functional situations and try to set up many small church communities of people who are in the same situation. There could be special situational frameworks within the Church, not only for the spheres of responsibility in which people work, but also for groups of people of the same intellectual level or of the same age (young people, old people, etc.).

The great difficulty that is brought about by the territorial system is the expansion of any given church community into an anonymous mass. Because people happen to live in a given residential district, they are, as members of the Church, simply thrown together and artificially raised to the level of a "community". This inevitably leads to frustration in the proclamation of the Christian message, which has to be aimed at an indiscriminate mass of people that must nonetheless be treated as a whole. The consequence is that the preacher is forced to speak in such a way that what he says can be understood by the group with the lowest intelligence. This in turn frequently results in a real crisis of faith among the more intelligent, the better educated and the academically minded who are longing for solid food, but have to put up with milk. This undoubtedly accounts for the spontaneous formation of small discussion groups in the

Netherlands with the aim of discussing the faith at a deeper level. I believe that this is at the same time an indication of a spontaneous desire for small church communities which could aim to become fully conscious of the consequences of Christian faith within their specific situation.

Bishops and parish priests will in future have to direct their attention far more to situational church communities, rather than to an indiscriminate mass of people brought together by chance within a given territory. And this will, incidentally, mean a great saving in money spent on expensive church buildings. The small church community of the future kenotic Church can, after all, assemble and celebrate the Eucharist in any suitable place.

The Local Church Community

It will already be clear from what I have said in the foregoing section that the local church community will in future have to play an increasingly important part. One of the difficulties contained in the conciliar decree on the Church is that in it New Testament texts are applied to the present situation with insufficiently subtle distinction.

In primitive Christianity, the word "bishop" had quite a different meaning from what it has now. The bishop in the New Testament was not the head of a territorial diocese, but of a local church *community*.[1] Had this fact been better known, the local church community would have been accorded a more important place at the Council than it in fact was.

The local church community of the future will have to be small. Its members will know each other personally and will often work and live in similar spheres. They will be dedicated to their small community and regard it as part of the whole Church. Strongly conscious of their mission, they will equip themselves in their small community to make their Christian view of humanity and the future of the world effective in their decisions within the structures of society.

They will be fully committed to taking an active part in

132

human history, and they will constantly measure the existing situation in the world against the reality of the "new creation" and the new humanity (2 Cor. 5. 17).

"Persevering in one Mind" (see Acts 1.14)

It is obvious that, if there are to be many local church communities, there will also be considerable pluriformity in the Church. Fear of losing her unity has prompted the Church to make an almost unique principle of uniformity. But uniformity is an aspect of the Church's form of power, because it is the principle underlying the control of humanity as a mass. This is impressive, but it lacks depth. The human race is not simply a homogeneous mass. It consists of individuals and groups at many different levels. The Church must recognize this and adapt herself to it.

Although the broad basic structure of the Church's liturgy will remain the same everywhere, there will be increasing pluriformity in liturgical expression and experience as the local church communities develop and, in addition to this, a corresponding pluriformity in theology. This pluriformity is undoubtedly an essential aspect of a Church that is orientated towards a pluriform human race and pluriform human situations. A modern ecclesiologist, such as Dr J. Mulders, S.J., clearly realized this when he wrote:

There are, of course, certain basic elements which form part of the essence of the Church and which must as such also be visible. These include, for example, the celebration of the Eucharist and preaching about Jesus as the Lord. But these basic elements are, so to speak, made visible in the second power—the essential rite of the Eucharist is included in an entirety of words and actions, an important part of which is determined by more local and historical circumstances. The eucharistic texts in Paul and Luke, for example, deviate, in their ritual, from the traditions of Matthew and Mark. This law emerges very clearly in the theology of the New Testament. The Johannine Christology differs from the Pauline—faith in the one Lord (Eph. 4. 4-6) is incarnated in different theologies. The same phenomenon is also apparent in the development of the Church. *The existence of pluriformity around the one nucleus is an essential element of the Church.* Or, to put it more accurately, the one nucleus exists *in* pluriformity.[2]

There is, of course, the possible objection that this pluriformity contains a danger to the unity of the Church. My reply to this is that uniformity does not in itself bring about unity. The unity of the Church is a unanimity, a single-mindedness, a unity of heart and soul, of faith and confession and of mutual love. It is therefore important to stress that the local church community is not an independent "church", but must be *in communio* with the larger local community, the head of which is the "overseer", the bishop.

The bishop's most important task is to ensure that unity in faith is preserved among the multiplicity of forms, although it is perhaps even more important for this unity in faith to be expressed in the unity of mutual love. The existence of many pluriform local church communities could easily give rise to "class distinctions" within the Church. The bishop must see to it that the unity of brotherly love is preserved between the churches. Representatives of the various churches will therefore have to come together from time to time in order to manifest, in eucharistic solidarity, the unity of the greater local church community of the diocese.

But the bishop and his diocese also do not constitute an independent, enclosed group. Each bishop is a bishop only because he belongs to the community, the college, of Catholic bishops. Joseph Ratzinger has expressed it, with reference to the early Church, in the following way:

The bishop in himself is not the successor of one single apostle. It is the college of bishops which continues the college of the apostles, and the individual bishop is within the apostolic succession because he belongs to this college. Thus, togetherness with the other bishops is important for the individual bishop. . . . But the togetherness of the bishops at the same time includes the togetherness and the inter-communion of the separate communities, through which they together form the one *Ecclesia*, although they are outwardly many.[3]

The mutual unity of the college of bishops is finally given its decisive point of orientation and its "personal summit" (to use Karl Rahner's phrase) in the bishop of Rome. In this way, the structure of the Church's unanimity, her singlemindedness, her unity of heart and soul and her unity of faith, hope and love is guaranteed, despite the multiplicity of forms and the differences between the communities in which these are expressed.

Wide perspectives are opened up by this principle of pluriformity for the spread of the gospel among non-European peoples. It should no longer be necessary to impose the religious forms of the West on people with a totally different cultural background. Pluriformity should also provide a solution to the problem of the unequal development of the Church and religion in the world. It was to some extent unfair to impose the vernacular liturgy on more traditional and conservative church communities without preparing them for this. If people are not ready to accept a new liturgical form, it should not be suddenly imposed on them. The Council was well aware of the unequal development within the Church and decided to retain the Latin canon as a compromise solution. But this also meant that many of the more progressive communities in the Church felt that they had received a serious check. These difficulties should be solved at once if the principle of single-mindedness in pluriformity is accepted.

The Clergy

What is to be the relationship between the clergy and the laity in the kenotic Church? If we are really to understand this problem, we must consider the situation in the Church before the "choice" of the fourth century. At that time, the only difference between the clergy and the laity was one of *function* within the Church.

Certain of the lay members of the local church were chosen and ordained to perform a certain function in the Church. They are, however, no longer in fact chosen and called from the community itself. The following correct, but extremely minimal formulation was made by the Council of Trent: "In the consecration of bishops and the ordination of priests, the consent of, or the calling by the people is not demanded in the sense that the consecration or ordination would be invalid without this consent or call."[4] This calling by the church community ceased later to be practised and all that remains of it now is a formality in the rites of consecration and ordination. This "calling" to office in the Church has become a kind of mystical experience on the part of the individual, who feels that he has been directly "called" by God.

I believe that we must first revert to this choice and calling by the church community itself of one of their number to fulfil the office of preaching the gospel and administering the sacraments.

Secondly, this function must be freed from everything that has made the clergy into a privileged class. The bishops and priests of the Church of power acquired all kinds of privileges which enhanced their honour and prestige. "These privileges are part of the body of legal measures which henceforward contributed their share towards making the clergy a class apart. Among these measures, celibacy was one of the most important, but others, such as the introduction of a special costume . . . effectually initiated a considerable change in the relations between the faithful and the presidents of the community, priests or bishops."[5] In 428, Pope Celestine I censured Honoratus, the abbot of Lérins, who had become bishop of Atrecht (or Arras), for introducing special clothing—the tunic and belt that were worn by monks. He would not tolerate such novelties. Up to that time, *priests had been in no way distinguishable from other men* and even when they celebrated the liturgy they simply put on "clean clothes". Celestine therefore wrote to the bishops in the district of Narbonne: "Let us be distinguished from others by our knowledge, not by our dress and by our conversation, not by our striking exterior."[6]

In order to give the privileged position of the clergy an exalted spiritual character, certain monastic rules of life were also prescribed for the secular clergy. Office in the Church, which was originally a functional duty within the church community, later became a privileged position with a special spiritual way of life. This completed the division between the clergy and the laity—and the isolation of the clergy that accompanied this division.

In the kenotic Church, we shall have to return to the original form of office-bearer who, as far as his outward appearance and his standard of life are concerned, is in no way distinguishable from the other members of the church community. There remains the difficulty of celibacy. This will therefore have to be abolished for those holding office in the Church. By this I mean that the state of virginity should continue to exist in the Church, but that it should not necessarily be associated with the clerical office. A measure of this kind would at once relieve the great shortage of priests. Many qualified laymen who are already married could then be called to the function of office in the Church.

Until now, women have not been permitted to hold office in the Church. This, however, is a way of thinking which dates back to an older pattern of society that was dominated by men. There is no theological objection to admitting women to office in the Church. In our modern society, in which women have—formally at least—equal rights with men, there can be no objection to calling women as well to certain suitable functions of the one office in the Church. If this office means above all "service" and "care" for sacrament and word in the Church, then it is here a question of qualities which would traditionally seem to fit women more than men. I can therefore imagine that women could be called to the ministry of the word and that they would seem to be particularly well suited to administer baptism (to children) and the sacrament of the anointing of the sick.

The Laity

It will only be possible for those Christians who are now known as "lay" people to become fully aware of their real mission and task in the Church when the office of the clergy has been "emptied".

Etymologists tell us that the word "lay" is derived from the Greek *laos*, a word meaning "people".[7] Laymen and women are not in any way secondary members of the Church. They are quite simply the *laos theou*—the people of God, in other words, the Church. As the responsible *laos* (laity), they are practically the only ones who can carry out the service of the Church in a society which is dominated by "powers". A clericalized Church composed of active priests and passive lay members may have the outward appearance of a Church, but it takes no part in the world and is consequently not the People of God in the world.[8]

I am not referring here to what has been called the "lay apostolate". For this movement has never succeeded in becoming a total commitment on the part of the whole People of God. Despite all attempts to make it a real work of the laity, it has never become anything more than an extension of the activity of the clergy. In it, the laity have simply been the assistants of the clergy. But, as the serving People of God, fully conscious of their mission, lay people in the Church are not the assistants of the clergy, helping the priests to do their work better. The priests are the assistants of the whole People of God, helping everyone to be the Church. Only the laity as the People of God can be effectively present in the creative centres of our society.

One very important task of the clergy in the future will therefore be to make the laity conscious of its call to service as the People of God within the structures of secular society. A number of qualified and conscious lay people will therefore have to be theologically trained. We shall indeed see a completely different form of theology arise when the teaching of theology is freed from the limitations and the isolation of the environment of the seminary.

It is in the secular structures that important decisions relating to individuals and society are taken. Lay Christians who are involved in these decisions in business life, economics, technology or politics are usually not aware of the fact that in all these spheres a certain image of man and society that is automatically and unquestioningly accepted is manipulated. The lay Christian has to measure these human presuppositions which are manipulated in the dynamic centres of our society against the Christian image of man, the Christian view of the future and the Christian idea of society as the New Creation and the New Humanity.

In this context, I should like to quote what Congar has said: "It seems that the presentation of religion primarily as worship and moral obligations, the classic heritage of the seventeenth century, deprived us in some ways of the realization that Christianity presents a *hope*, a total hope, even for the material world." And he continues: "The People of God is rediscovering once again that it possesses a messianic character and that it bears the hope of a fulfilment of the world in Jesus Christ. . . . Chosen, established, consecrated by God to be his *servant* and his witness, the People of God is, in the world, the sacrament of salvation offered to the world."[9]

The Religious Communities

Monastic life is also in a critical situation at the moment. This too is a result of the fact that we have lost sight of the origin of the religious way of life.

If we consider this origin rather schematically and without attention to detail, we may conclude that it was related to the charismatic witness of faith of the martyrs of the first Christian centuries. Martyrdom was a special witness of faith in a society that was hostile to Christianity. When this hostility changed into a positive acceptance of Christianity (in the fourth century!), the need was still felt in the Church for some form of special testimony and monastic life developed from the anchoretic way of life into a *way of life* practised by a community which aimed to bear a special and charismatic witness to the faith in the Church and the world. The monastic community was, as it were, an intensification of the greater community of the Church, a reflection of the ideal Church, and as such an exalted witness to the life of faith and love in that Church.

In later centuries, when luxury, politics and a love of pleasure began to predominate in the Church, more and more emphasis was placed in the monastic life on poverty, simplicity and penitence (the mendicant orders). Francis of Assisi and his followers were probably the first to express the longing of Christians for a return to the kenotic Church in their way of life. Something of the kenotic Church was also reflected in another aspect of monastic life—the rich variety of this life and the many small communities were, of course, an image of the many pluriform local church communities, each with their own *episkopos* (the abbot, prior or superior) at the head. Historically speaking, then, what we see in monastic life is a constant seeking for the kenotic Church.

Monastic life also developed its own special "status"—the status or state of perfection. Whenever the clergy—which soon came to be known as the "secular" clergy, so as to distinguish its members from the monks or "regulars"— became spiritually decadent, the monks were called upon to renew the spiritual state (Cluny, the mendicant orders, the Jesuits and so on). A certain tension arose between the clergy and the monastic orders, with the result that both "states" were influenced by each other.

Although those holding office in the Church had previously been distinguished from the rest of the faithful only by their special duties and function, the privileged status of the clergy which developed later led to a different way of life learnt from the monks. The renewal set in motion by the Council of Trent also led to reform in the training of priests. Many seminaries were set up under the direction of the new Society of Jesus. The priestly way of life was henceforward strongly influenced by Ignatian spirituality. (This is still noticeable in the Church's present-day canon law.)

On the other hand, monastic life was more and more influenced by the pastoral needs of the Church, with the result that more and more monks were ordained. It very rarely happens nowadays that a monk is not at the same time a priest. In the eighteenth and nineteenth centuries, a great number of Congregations were founded and these were in fact active communities of priests whose work was pastoral although their structure was monastic and based on the religious way of life. As religious, these men committed themselves to a monastic rule, a special, regulated way of life which suggested life "within" the monastery. But as priests, they were obliged, because of the pastoral needs of the Church, to go "outside" the community and thus compelled to lead a very different way of life. The active priest-religious had to lead, in other words, an ambivalent life.

If the religious life is to be renewed, then here too there must be a "return". The immediate shortage of priests will become less acute if the seculars are no longer required to be celibate and, in that case, many of the regular priests in religious orders will be able to withdraw from the practice of the Church's pastoral office and devote themselves to their real task in the Church. They must be a constant manifestation of the Church as Christ wished her to be, a constant and special witness of the faith and a special local church community which is a light for the one *Ecclesia* and for the world. I shall discuss the further content and meaning of this later.

So far, I have said nothing about the religious orders for women. It is, of course, obvious that the contemplative orders of women, whose way of life was patterned on that of the monks (they were therefore called *moniales*), have been less affected by clerical tendencies than the male religious orders. The female religious communities, however, flourished in the eighteenth and nineteenth centuries and many of these were employed in various tasks concerned with pastoral care, such as teaching and the care of the sick and the aged. But, as these tasks have been gradually taken over by the State social services, women in religious communities have become increasingly uncertain about what they are to do and how they are to justify their own existence. On the other hand, many of those in contemplative orders have been wanting more and more to be employed in one way or another in active pastoral work.

All this is indicative of a search for "origins". And may we not suppose that this is at the same time a search for kenotic experience? May it not be that men and women in religious communities have a special task in leading the way towards the Church's kenotic form of service? I shall have more to say about this in a different connection later in this chapter. In the meantime, another aspect of the kenotic Church must be discussed.

Church Order

Life in a community of believers has, of course, to be regulated according to a definite legal order. This order has, up till now, been set out in a code of ecclesiastical law (the *Codex Iuris Canonici*), modelled on Roman law. But Roman law is a constitutional law, and we are bound to question whether the system of law of a kenotic Church has to be based on principles of the constitutional law of a State.

In her task of service, the Church must not set her own system of law beside or above the system of civil law if this ecclesiastical law is formed on an analogy with the structure and principles of the law of a State. If the fundamental freedom and rights of man are infringed (as, for example, in the choice of a partner in marriage), then we are bound to ask whether the Church can declare the actions of her faithful to be valid or invalid, or whether she can make the persons concerned competent or incompetent to do acts or to take decisions.[10]

In principle, the starting-point for the Church's legal order should be the local church community. According to the principles of pluriformity, the legal system of a local church community cannot, of course, be regulated in detail. But rules could certainly be given which would establish what is necessary to the functioning of the local community. More concrete regulations could be left to the discretion of the bishop. So far, everything has always been regulated "from above". Now, however, these higher authorities—the bishops, the bishops' conferences, the Pope and so on—should act as authorities to whom appeal could be made. Whenever there is, for example, conflict in a local church or doubt about matters of faith and life, an appeal could be made to a higher authority, beginning with the bishop and, if necessary, going as far as the Pope.

The new Church order must draw its inspiration and emanate far more from the pastoral office in the Church.

The Church as a "Zone of Truth"

A brief summary of a speech made in Berlin in July 1964 by Josef Pieper will explain what I mean by "zone of truth". Almost the whole of this speech was printed in the *Frankfurter Allgemeine Zeitung* of the 29 July 1964 under the title "Der Verderb des Wortes und die Macht" ("The Corruption of the Word and Power").[11]

Pieper takes as his starting-point the apparently academic question, what was Plato's precise objection to the Sophists? Plato brought many different charges against the Sophists, and all of them apply strictly to our contemporary situation. One of his accusations was their "corruption of the word" (*Korrumpierung des Wortes*). An element of human existence is contained in the word and, if the word is corrupted, human existence cannot remain inviolate. The Sophists, Plato maintained, corrupted the word, which, in their teaching, no longer had the function of communicating truth, but was simply manipulated for the purpose of making an impression, without regard for the truth. This resulted in the other person ceasing to be a real partner in dialogue and becoming merely an object—human *material*—to be used by the speaker. The word thus lost its communicative character and became a means of power, a weapon.

There are countless examples of the enormous extent to which our contemporary society is permeated, as Plato's was, by the sophistic use of the word. In advertising, the word is used with calculated effect, with an eye to its possible success. This is constantly happening in politics, in which the word is frequently debased to the level of a flattering slogan and, in the extreme case of a régime of terror, it can become a dangerous weapon. In such cases, and in others, the degradation of language is always a degradation of communication, of real human community.

A final answer which Plato gave to the question that so preoccupied him was made in this formulation: "The Sophist is a maker of fictive reality" (*"Der Sophist ist ein Verfertiger fiktiver Realität"*). The Sophist was, in other words, not concerned with truth—in its place, he put an apparent reality.

This sentence of Plato's can also be applied with appalling pertinence to our contemporary situation. It is true of the modern entertainment industry, of the sensational press and often of politics or all that is taken for granted in the hidden ideology of our society, all of which make use of "fictive reality" and all of which have, not the aim of communicating truth, but of offering us something that we can swallow easily and with pleasure. This fictive reality is so prevalent in our society that the average man is not only not able to find the true reality, but also not even able to look for it. His vision is so limited to this fictive reality that he is no longer able to look beyond and above it.

At the end of his speech, Pieper has some very worthwhile things to say in defence of our existence against sophistic tendencies of this kind today. One of these things is that there must be a "zone of truth" in our society where men can be concerned with truth quite apart from any aim or intention. Because he was speaking at a University gathering, he suggested that the University should be this "zone of truth".

Without wishing to dispute this, I should also like to suggest that the Church should primarily show the deeper dimension of her service and ministry as the sacrament of salvation in our society by being the *zone of truth*. I am also convinced that the Church can carry out this function only very imperfectly in her imperial form of power because, in a situation of power, her own prestige is always at stake.

Truthfulness

Kenōsis means that the Church must empty herself of all false desire for prestige. By false prestige, I mean not only what was called "triumphalism" at the Council, but also the attitude that the impression that the Church makes on the outside world must *at all costs* be preserved. A distinction is therefore made between the individual Catholic and the Church. The individual can err, sin, forfeit grace and so on, but the Church cannot. In this way, it was possible to speak of a "Church of sinners", but not of a "sinful Church" (the whore of Babylon). This distinction seemed at one time to provide a solution to many difficulties, but it is becoming more and more difficult to maintain in the light of the changes and the changed views in the present Church.

The Pope, however, made a confession of guilt *in the name of the Church* at the Council (even though this was expressed in the subjunctive mood). If the Church has indeed been guilty, then she has really failed—as the Church! All the same, there is still a tendency, even where drastic changes are taking place, to stress *continuity* above all. The changes are certainly happening, but the Church does not really go back on anything.[12] There is a distinct fear of giving rise to the possible impression that the Church has *erred* in the past. The papal encyclicals are not "infallible statements made *ex cathedra*", but they are surrounded by an aura of infallibility, so that it is always difficult to admit at a later period that they were determined by existing historical conditions and are now, in the light of our present experience, untenable or even erroneous. To admit this, however, might damage the Church's prestige. It is impossible not to feel that an acknowledgement by the Church of her own mistakes and misconceptions is regarded as highly dangerous to her, with the result that every attempt is made to show that there is *continuity* in all the changes that are taking place.

I, however, believe that a kenotic Church, going forward in service and humility and always open to truthful self-criticism in the light of the gospel and any new historical situation, will increase her "prestige" rather than harm it.

This brings us to the question of the Church's honesty and truthfulness. One of the greatest difficulties in ecumenical dialogue is the impression of untrustworthiness that the Roman Catholic Church always appears to make. It is true that there is a tremendous number of very honest individual Catholics, but is the Church as a whole so sincere? Outsiders find it difficult to trust the Church of smooth-tongued, diplomatic prelates and cunning, hair-splitting theologians who, with all kinds of fine distinctions, demonstrate that the Church has *never really* made any mistakes.

Nothing has damaged the trustworthiness of the Catholic Church so much in the eyes of those who think differently (and in the eyes of the modern world in general) as the Church's refusal to admit mistakes that have been made and her hushing up, obscuring or reasoning her way out of these errors. Surely it is in this context remarkable that, in the Church's traditional moral theology, sins against the sixth commandment have always (in themselves) been regarded as grave sins, whereas those against the eighth commandment —sins against truthfulness—have been classified as venial sins? The truth of the Church is intimately bound up with her truthfulness. To be a "zone of truth" means that the Church must constantly verify the ideologies of the world and the way of life that goes with them. She must therefore be intensely present in the world, but she must at the same time preserve sufficient space to be able to stand aside in order not to be drawn powerlessly into and dragged along by the secular dynamism.

As I have already said, the life movement of Christianity cannot, in the last resort, be synchronized with the movement of the world as expressed in the dynamism of modern society. The fictive reality which modern society painlessly and almost imperceptibly forces upon us must be recognized *as fictive*. The one-sidedness and limitation of the hidden view of the world which can so cramp the spirit must be revealed. The deepest questions about man must continue to be asked and the healthy unrest of Christian sobriety and watchfulness must be kept alive. It is impossible to be a believer now in a small, private and inviolable enclave—we are all believers *in the world*. Truth and appearance, honesty and lies are not present in a pure form in this world. Appearance is presented as truth and lies are presented as honesty. It is the constant task of the Church as the "zone of truth" to unmask this.

To fulfil a task such as this requires an ability to *see* with this sense especially sharpened by faith. It is obviously not a task that can be performed by everyone, but it does seem to me that it could be done by the religious orders in the Church. These have always had the tendency to withdraw themselves from the world. This has sometimes led, unfortunately, to a complete and false isolation. In my view, those in religious orders are called to be on the one hand completely present in the world and, on the other, to some extent withdrawn. Their presence should thus be a presence with some reservation. This distance is necessary if they are to reflect about the deeper movement of life in our world and then, by reflection, to see the real motivation of our contemporary society in the light of the gospel and reveal it.

A great deal more could, of course, be said about the concrete forms that the accomplishment of this task must take, but I will do no more here than simply point out that I believe that this could be a genuine sphere of apostolic activity for many of the religious orders that are at present looking for a new meaning for their existence and a new form of work. This sphere of work is, moreover, not so contrary as it may at first appear to the original purpose of the religious communities in the Church. It is, after all, only in true service to the truthfulness of a kenotic Church that it will be possible to continue the work of Christ in deep faith. He who said "I am the truth" was tireless in seeing through and exposing all false appearances, insincerity and whitewashed tombs. His task was to destroy the hidden "powers" (1 Cor. 15. 24).

Conclusion

In this chapter I have simply given, in broad outline, some of the concrete consequences of our acceptance of a kenotic Church. What I have suggested may seem to be very radical changes, but I have not really altered anything of the Church's essence. All that I have done is to draw on the infinite riches of the Church's *radix*. I am utterly convinced that a kenotic Church is a much more eloquent witness to the mystery of Christ than a Church of imperial power.

A kenotic Church is also much less vulnerable than an imperial Church. In her kenotic form, the Church is far more able to withdraw from the mastery of the ideological "powers" that are concealed within the patterns of our modern society and is thus less tangible. Her activity would originate in and spread from the unpretentious spheres of small local communities rather than a powerful central-ized authority. A kenotic Church would no longer need to be engaged in a constant struggle for existence in modern society, a struggle to preserve her own structures of influ-ence. She would thus be far more able to pursue her work in societies which were hostile to her or which persecuted her. To express it in military terms, her strategy would be pluriform and mobile.

Only a kenotic Church can be really ecumenical. The greatest obstacle to dialogue with the other Christian churches and communities was the Catholic Church's form of power. It was precisely this power that originally formed the chief protest of the reformers. Ecumenical dialogue will be placed on an entirely new footing with the disappearance of the Church's power, and I am even inclined to suspect that forms of really ecclesial unity will be discovered at the level of the local churches.

A kenotic Church will also make the spread of the gospel on a world-wide scale possible for the first time.[13] The Church in the form of service will no longer be bound to Western forms of Christianity and will be able to be present, as a servant, in the non-Christian cultures of Asia and Africa and to make use of all the achievements of these cultures A kenotic Church has no exclusive claims to revelation and grace. She will have reverence for the mystery of God's revelation and grace present in the religious heritage and experience of the non-Christian religions.

One final question still remains to be answered—how is this change of direction towards the kenotic Church to be accomplished? It will certainly not be brought about by any "measures" or by reorganization. It will above all be the result of a *metanoia*, a change of heart or conversion, the development of a new mentality, a kenotic attitude. Anyone who listens to what is being said among the higher and lower clergy and among those who are called the "laity" will be conscious of a more or less explicit longing everywhere for the kenotic Church. The struggle against triumphalism and juridicism and the longing for the "Church of the poor" at the Council—what were these but an expression of a forward-looking desire on the part of Christians for a different form of the Church?—a Church of *kenōsis* and of the Servant of Yahweh? It is therefore a question of a new attitude and I can, in conclusion, only repeat the words of the apostle Paul: "Have this mind among yourselves, which you have in Christ Jesus . . . who emptied himself, taking the form of a servant." (Phil. 2. 5, 7).

Epilogue

The gospels speak of two kinds of grave.

One was whitewashed, the other was empty.

The whitewashed grave is the symbol of the false façade, of the outwardly beautiful appearance that does not last.

The empty grave was the grave of the God-man, Jesus Christ, the one who was himself emptied.

The hope of the future was born around that emptiness.

People stared into the empty grave. They were reminded not to look for the living among the dead.

Then the cry went up, he is alive—he has risen! More and more people gathered and were baptized in the name of Jesus Christ for the forgiveness of their sins. They devoted themselves earnestly to the apostles' teaching and fellowship, to the breaking of bread and to prayer.

This was the Church.

Thus, around the emptiness of the grave were born both the hope of the future and the Church, which was, is and must always be *the Message of what is to come.*

Notes

Introduction

1. See my book *The Church is Different* (London and New York, 1966).
2. Dr J. M. van der Veen, "Kerk en toekomst", in *Wending*, 20 (1965), pp. 649-50.
3. *Universitas-schrift*, 10 (Louvain, 1965).
4. See Dom Aelred Graham, "The Pathos of Vatican II", in *Encounter*, 25 (1965), no. 6, pp. 16-22.
5. *Op. cit.*, pp. 65-71.
6. "All of them were theologians on the march, men well equipped with ideas that dovetailed neatly into the needs of the pastors around the world." Robert Kaiser, *Inside the Council* (London, 1963).

Chapter I

1. Friedrich Nietzsche, *Die fröhliche Wissenschaft. Gesammelte Werke*, XII, pp. 156-7 (Musarion Verlag, Munich, 1924).
2. Gabriel Vahanian, *The Death of God* (New York, 1961). By the same author, *Wait without Idols* (New York, 1964).
3. William Hamilton, *The New Essence of Christianity* (New York, 1961), p. 58 ff.
4. Thomas J. J. Altizer, *Mircea Eliade and the Dialectic of the Sacred* (Philadelphia, 1963). A summary of Hamilton's and Altizer's ideas is given in their *Radical Theology and the Death of God* (New York, 1966).
5. *Op. cit.*, p. 13. The italics are Altizer's.
6. Paul van Buren, *The Secular Meaning of the Gospel* (London, 1963).
7. A. Vergote, *Universitas-schrift*, 10 (Louvain, 1965).
8. Walter Schultz, "Der Gott der modernen Metaphysik", *Der Gottesgedanke im Abendland* (Stuttgart, 1964), pp. 89-108.
9. H. Berkhof, "Theologiseren in een a-theïstisch tijdperk", *Katernen 2000*, no. 2 (Amersfoort, 1965).
10. A good summary of the philosophical problem of God and of the misuse that can be made of an objectivized "God" can be found in W. Luijpen, *Fenomenologie en Atheïsme* (Utrecht, 1963).
11. "Herinterpretatie van het geloof in het licht van de seculariteit", in *Tijdschrift voor Theologie*, 4 (1964), pp. 148-9.
12. See Edwin M. Good, "The Meaning of Demythologization", in *The Theology of Rudolf Bultmann*, ed. Charles W. Kegley (New York, 1966), pp. 21-44.
13. In the strict sense of the word, Heidegger is not an existentialist, but an ontologist. In his analysis of the structures of being of human existence (*Daseinsanalyse*), his point of departure is the problem of being.

14. Paul Tillich, *Systematic Theology*, Introduction, Vol. 1 (London, 1953), p. 3-10.

15. See note 6.

16. *Op. cit.*, p. 17.

17. *Op. cit.*, p. 14.

CHAPTER II

1. Richard F. Behrendt, *Der Mensch im Licht der Soziologie* (Stuttgart, 1962).

2. Fritz Gummert, quoted in Werner Conze, *Die Strukturgeschichte des technisch-industriellen Zeitalters als Aufgabe für Forschung und Unterricht* (Cologne, 1957).

3. See the essay "The Futurists", *Time*, Vol. 87 (1966), no. 8, pp. 22-3. See also *Unsere Welt 1985*, ed. Robert Jungk (Vienna, 1965) and A. Th. van Leeuwen, "Globaal Perspectief", *Wending*, 20 (1965), pp. 533-44.

4. See, for example, Harvey Cox, *The Secular City* (New York and London, 1965) and *God's Revolution and Man's Responsibility* (Valley Forge, Pa., 1965); the authors of *The Triple Revolution*; Fred. I. Polak, *Automatie als doorbraak naar nieuwe internationale verhoudingen* (Amersfoort, 1965).

5. Robert Adolfs, *op. cit.*, pp. 123-9.

6. Harvey Cox has set out in an excellent manner the implications of urbanization for the Church and Christianity in his book *The Secular City*.

7. Harvey Cox, *op. cit.*, p. 121.

8. Peter Hall, *The World Cities* (London, 1966),

9. An immense number of books has been written about urbanization. Apart from the works that I have already mentioned, I have consulted Kingsley Davis' illuminating, but statistically out of date article "The Origin and Growth of Urbanization in the World", *The American Journal of Sociology*, Vol. LX (1955), pp. 429-37; Amos H. Hawley, *Human Ecology* (New York, 1950), pp. 239-45; Brian J. L. Berry and W. L. Garrison, *Recent Developments in Central Place Theory* (Papers and Proceedings of the Regional Science Association, 1958); Edgar M. Hoover, "The Concept of a System of Cities", *Economic Development and Cultural Change*, Vol. III (1955); Otis Dudley Duncan *et al.*, *Metropolis and Region* (Baltimore, 1960), pp. 259-75; Alvin Boskoff, *The Sociology of Urban Regions* (New York, 1962); Jean Gottmann, *Megalopolis* (New York, 1961).

10. Richard F. Behrendt, "Weltbevölkerungsprobleme", *Echo der Welt*, Vol. III (Zurich, 1959), pp. 25 ff.

11. These data have been taken from Joseph A. Davis' article, "Population", in *The Fabric of Society*, ed. Ralph Ross and Ernest van der Haag (New York, 1957), pp. 434-41.

12. Karl Sax, *Standing Room Only* (Boston, 1955).

13. For data on this subject, I have drawn chiefly on three numbers of *Katernen 2000*, published by Werkgroep 2000, Amersfoort: *Katern* 1, "De drievoudige revolutie"; *Katern* 3, Dr Fred. I. Polak (see note 4); *Katern* 4/5, Donald N. Michael, "Problemen rond Automatisering". I have also consulted George Paloczi-Horvath, *The Facts Rebel* (London, 1964); Norbert Wiener, "The Human Use of Human Beings", *Cybernetics and Society* (London and New York, 1950); *idem*, "Some Moral and Technical Consequences of Automation", *Science*, Vol. 131 (1960), no. 3410; John Diebold,

Automation: Its Impact on Business and Labor, Planning Pamphlet no. 106 (Washington, 1959).

14. *Op. cit.*, pp. 11 and 12.

15. *Op. cit.*, p. 35.

16. "The Human Use of Human Beings" (see note 13), p. 213.

17. Karl Jaspers, *Vom Ursprung und Ziel der Geschichte* (Munich, 1949), p. 178.

18. R. F. Behrendt, *Der Mensch im Licht der Soziologie, op. cit.*, p. 97.

19. B. Landheer, *Beeld van de toekomst* (Rotterdam, 1965), pp. 68 ff.

20. See John T. Robinson, *The New Reformation?* (London, 1965), p. 88.

CHAPTER III

1. This is the general drift of the article "Toekomstig Christendom", *De Heraut*, 96 (1965), pp. 141-53.

2. See J. Mulders, S.J., *Het mysterie der kerk* (Tielt and The Hague, 1965), pp. 19, 20.

3. J. Ratzinger, "Het kerkbegrip der Vaders", *DO-C Dossier* no. 4 (Hilversum, 1965), pp. 27, 28.

4. For the following, I am indebted to Gibson Winter, *The New Creation as Metropolis* (New York, 1963). By the same author, *The Suburban Captivity of the Churches* (Garden City, 1961). See also P. E. Kraemer, "Kerk-in-antwoord is kerk-in-situatie", *Gemeente in Meervoud* (Amsterdam, 1965), pp. 11-25.

5. P. E. Kraemer, *op. cit.*, pp. 22 and 23.

6. *The Suburban Captivity of the Churches, op. cit.*, p. 136.

7. G. W. F. Hegel, *Grundlinien der Philosophie des Rechts*, ed. J. Hoffmeister (Hamburg, 1955) (the first edition of this book appeared in 1821), par. 188, p. 169. See also J. Ritter, *Hegel und die französische Revolution* (Hamburg, 1957), pp. 36 ff.

8. *Op. cit.*, par. 187, pp. 167-8.

9. *Op. cit.*, par. 209, p. 180.

10. A. Gehlen, "Mensch trotz Masse", *Wort und Wahrheit*, 7 (1952), pp. 579 ff.

11. H. Schelsky, *Die skeptische Generation* (Düsseldorf, 1963), p. 297.

12. Harvey Cox, *The Secular City, op. cit.*, p. 46. See the whole passage pp. 38-49.

13. F. Gogarten, *Der Mensch zwischen Gott und Welt* (Stuttgart, 1952), p. 181 ff.

14. R. Bultmann, *Glauben und Verstehen*, III (Tübingen, 1962), p. 196.

15. R. Bultmann, "Der Gottesgedanke und der moderne Mensch", *Zeitschrift für Theologie und Kirche*, 60 (1963), pp. 335 ff. This article also appears in the collection, *Der Christ in der neuen Wirklichkeit* (Frankfurt, 1964), pp. 11-21.

16. Gerhard Ebeling, *Theologie und Verkündigung* (Tübingen, 1962), p. 101.

17. A. Th. van Leeuwen, *Christianity in World History* (Edinburgh, 1964), p. 410.

18. Par. 65, 91, 174.

19. I do not, of course, deny that suffering, sickness and death belong to the sphere of pastoral care in the Church.

20. A. Gehlen, *Urmensch und Spätkultur* (Düsseldorf, 1956), p. 69.

21. J. Sperna Weiland, "Geloof in geschiedenis", *Wending*, 21 (1966), p. 10.

22. "The relationship between faith and secularization is therefore such that there is no faith without the secularization of the relationship of the believer to the world", *op. cit.*, p. 141.

23. Johannes B. Metz, "Weltverständnis im Glauben", *Geist und Leben*, 35 (1962), pp. 165-84; *idem.*, "Zukunft des Glaubens in einer hominisierten Welt", *Hochland*, 56 (1964), pp. 377-91.

24. See note 17.

25. H. Schlier, *Principalities and Powers in the New Testament* (London and New York, 1961).

26. *Op. cit.*, p. 31.

27. *Op. cit.*, pp. 23-9.

28. See Pierre Berton, *The Comfortable Pew* (Philadelphia and London, 1965).

29. M. Merleau-Ponty, *Sens et non-sens* (Paris, 1948). This passage should be read in its context, pp. 305-21.

CHAPTER IV

1. See J. Mulders, *Het Mysterie der Kerk* (Tielt, 1965), Chapter II; L.G.M. Alting von Geusau, "Enkele aantekeningen over de Ecclesiologie, *DO-C* Dossier no. 4 (Hilversum, 1965), pp. 31-41; Michael Schmaus, *Katholische Dogmatik* (Munich, 1958), III, 1, pp. 202-96.

2. K. Barth, *Kirchliche Dogmatik*, Bd. IV, pp. 727-8.

3. See 1 Cor. 3. 6-9, 9-11, 16 and 17; Gal. 4. 26; 2 Cor. 11. 2; 1 Tim. 3. 5-15.

4. J. Ratzinger, "Over het kerkbegrip der Vaders", *DO-C Dossier* no. 4 (1965), p. 22.

5. H. de Lubac, *Corpus Mysticum* (Paris, 1949).

6. In addition to the Constitution on the Church (*Lumen Gentium*), I have also consulted J. Mulders' work (see note 1) and Y. Congar's article, "The Church : The People of God", in *Concilium*, 1, 1 (1965), pp. 7-20.

7. Acts 15. 14; 18. 10; 1 Pet. 2. 9; Tit. 2. 14.

8. I have devoted special attention to this idea in my book, *The Church is Different*, *op. cit.*, Chapters 1 and 6.

9. For this theme, see H. Urs von Balthasar, *Wer ist die Kirche?* (Basle, 1965), the chapter entitled "Die heilige Hure", pp. 55-137.

10. Cant. S 77, 1; Migne *PL* 183, 1156A.

11. See Michael Schmaus, *op. cit.*, pp. 684 ff.

12. The reader will, of course, realize that there is an analogy here with the problem discussed by Heidegger in connection with Western metaphysics. He also refers to a necessary "turning" (*Kehre*). Our problem has not been directly inspired by Heidegger, but the similarity occurred to me later. See S. IJsseling, "Het Zijn en de zijnden", *Tijdschrift voor Filosofie*, 28 (1966), pp. 3-53; cf. pp. 27-40.

13. Isa. 42. 1-9; 49. 1-11; 50. 4-11; 52. 13-53, 12.

14. I am indebted here to P. Schoonenberg's excellent article, "Kenosis", *Concilium*, 1, 2 (1966), pp. 27-36. For the exegesis, see also A. Feuillet, "L'Homme-Dieu considéré dans sa condition terrestre de Serviteur et de Redempteur", *Vivre et Penser*, 1 (1942), pp. 58-79.

15. P. Schoonenberg, *loc. cit.*, p. 28.

16. *Idem.*, p. 32.

17. *Idem.*, p. 34. My italics.

18. *Idem.*, pp. 35-36.

19. See John MacQuarrie, *An Existentialist Theology* (London, 1960), p. 215.

20. Ladislav Hajdanek, "Perspectieven van oecumenische arbeid in Tsjechoslowakije", *Kerk in Ontmoeting*, 2 (1966), p. 6.

21 See G. Auzou, *La Tradition biblique* (Paris, 1957), pp. 108 ff.

22. *Power and Poverty in the Church* (London and New York, 1964).

23. Yves Congar, *op. cit.*, pp. 12, 64, 64-5, 73 and 136-7.

24. "L'Ecclesiologie de saint Bernard", *Saint Bernard théologien, Anal. S. Ord. Cist.*, 9 (1953), p. 184.

25. *De Consideratione*, IV, 3. 6. Migne *PL*, 182, 776A.

26. Full texts of these and other statements on this subject are to be found in an appendix to Congar's book (see note 22 above).

27. See the American edition, *God's People on the March* (New York, 1966); This passage is not included in the British edition, *God's People on the Way* (London, 1966).

CHAPTER V

1. Among others, O. Cullmann has pointed this out in his article, "Die Bibel auf dem Konzil", *Evangelische Theologie*, 24 (1964), pp. 397-403.

2. J. Mulders, S.J., *Het Mysterie der Kerk, op. cit.*, p. 56. My italics.

3. J. Ratzinger, "Over het kerkbegrip der Vaders", *op. cit.*, p. 27.

4. Denz., 960 (1767-70).

5. Y. Congar, *op. cit.*, pp. 56-7.

6. *Epist.*, 4, 1, 2; Migne, *PL*, 50, 431.

7. I am aware that there are other possible etymological derivations.

8. Gibson Winter, *The New Creation as Metropolis, op. cit.*, p. 10 and 11.

9. Y. Congar, "The Church : The People of God"; *Concilium*, 1, 1 (1965), p. 10.

10. I have taken data here from a speech by L. C. Meijers, an official of the diocese of Den Bosch, about the possibilities and difficulties of mixed marriage. See the summary of this speech in *De Tijd*, 12 June 1966.

11. In this section, I am indebted to my fellow Augustinian, Dr J. B. Roeland, O.S.A., who drew my attention to Prof. Pieper's speech.

12. See Prof. G. C. Berkhouwer's four articles, "Het prestige der Kerk", *Gereformeerd Weekblad* 21 (1966), pp. 217, 225, 233 and 241.

13. See Dr C. A. van Peursen, C. Aalders and Dr J. Blauw, *Evangelieverkondiging in wereldperspectief* (Kampen, 1965).